PRACTICE
MAKES
PERFECT

Spanish Past-Tense Verbs
Up Close

Eric Vogt, Ph.D.

Mc
Graw
Hill

New York Chicago San Francisco Lisbon London Madrid Mexico City
Milan New Delhi San Juan Seoul Singapore Sydney Toronto

Contents

Overview of past tenses

Now and then

As you have studied Spanish, you have probably had the feeling that there are just too many past tenses. The frustration people encounter when they are trying to master the irregularities of the preterite can make some want to give up, or resign themselves to being speakers of one tense—the present.

Let pop psychology gurus say what they want about *living in the now*; in fact, we all *speak* in the now, in the sense that there is no other time in which we can exist. For grammatical purposes, the present is best viewed as a dot moving on a timeline—representing the moment or threshold of perception and utterance. Thus, the past is ever receding, with each moment of importance marked like so many telegraph poles on a desert highway seen from a speeding car.

We humans constantly report to each other what our day *was* like, or where we *were* when a world event happened, what our first date *was* like, or what *had already happened* by the time we got home. In order not to be misunderstood, we require an arsenal of past tenses, each with its particular relation to the present or to other moments in the past, in order to communicate background information or circumstances surrounding events in the past, or to tell our mother, spouse, or boss what had already happened to bring about those circumstances. We also need to be able to express what might have happened if events had been different. All of these subtleties are communicated in Spanish and English by the use of the various past tenses. Consider how much and how often we need to do this, *really* need to do this—to satisfy our own need to connect with each other. Once we realize the urgency of these complexities, it becomes clear how frighteningly dull the one-dimensionality of a present-tense world would be. Worse still, in some circumstances, if we only used the present tense the dangers of miscommunication could be truly life-threatening.

The past tenses we will examine in this book include the imperfect, preterite, present perfect, pluperfect, conditional, and conditional perfect, as well as the subjunctive forms of these tenses when subordinated to past tenses. Thus, following the first seven chapters, which cover the indicative forms of the past, chapter eight examines the imperfect subjunctive (i.e., simple, or one-word past subjunctive), the present perfect subjunctive, and the pluperfect subjunctive.

As with everything in foreign language learning, it isn't enough to grasp a concept or even to know the forms. One has to learn to use them when they are needed. Just as you can know the moves of chess pieces but miserably lose the game, you can know what you want to say, know the words and concepts you need to use, but fail to apply them all properly.

A little anecdote should suffice to convince you. I once conducted an oral placement test for a student who entered my office quite eager to get control of the situation by impressing me with a list of how many languages she could speak (as if it would matter when I listened to her try to speak the one I was there to test her in!). After a few simple questions in the present tense, which she answered quite confidently, I asked her a question about where she was when the Berlin Wall came down. At this she stopped and, looking at me with that look that deer have when confronted with an SUV on a dark highway, gathered her grammatical confidence and hastened to *explain*: "Oh, oh! I know! You need me to use the *preterite* and the *imperfect*! The *imperfect* is for where I was and the Berlin Wall coming down, that would be in the *preterite*!" She placed in the next-to-beginner's class—which was just fine. In such a class, her knowledge of the rules placed her in a slightly more advantageous position, but she still needed not only to acquire the vocabulary of infinitive verbs, but also to know their forms, regular and irregular, and all the other details that probably brought you to the bookshelf and inspired you to open this book.

So if you have been struggling to master the forms and uses of the different past tenses in Spanish, this book is for you. As you go through each section, testing yourself, reflecting on your errors, and reviewing all the while, also remember this: *explaining is not answering*. The student who came to my office could explain, but she could not answer. Students who are not secure in their knowledge of the details, their knowledge of forms and their uses, often fall into the trap of thinking that if they just grasp the rules about tense usage, they will be able to apply them when it is time to take the test. That just doesn't happen, any more than knowing black from white keys will help you play a piano. One symptom I have noticed, and all language teachers notice, too often, is that students who have only begun to digest their language learning will regurgitate verb conjugation patterns (often with telling errors) in the margins of their quizzes and tests. It is tempting, and we all understand it, but we also know that when students want to know the material in order to use it meaningfully, they will write it between their ears. I welcome you, as a reader of this book, to that category of dedicated learner.

The imperfect

Description and background

Of all the tenses in the Spanish language, the imperfect might be described as the most delightful. Although technically, the imperfect is one of two aspects of the past tense, the other being the preterite, we will use the common nomenclature and refer to them both as tenses, to keep things simple. The preterite and the imperfect are very commonly used together. Because these two aspects of the past are so important, each of them will first be examined alone, the imperfect in Chapter 1 and the preterite in Chapter 2, following which we will examine, in Chapter 3, the expressive power that comes from the ways in which the two are used together.

The imperfect is delightful to English-speaking learners of Spanish for at least four very good reasons. First, there are only *three* verbs in the entire language whose imperfect forms are irregular (**ser**, **ir**, and **ver**). Let's get them out of the way:

SER		IR		VER	
era	éramos	iba	íbamos	veía	veíamos
eras	erais	ibas	ibais	veías	veíais
era	eran	iba	iban	veía	veían

The imperfect of **hay** (the impersonal verb meaning *there is* or *there are*) is **había**, meaning *there was* or *there were*. Note that while **hay** itself is irregular, in the imperfect the form is actually regular, since it is derived from the helping verb **haber** (*to have*).

Secondly, there are just two sets of regular endings, one set for the **-ar** verbs and one set that the **-er** and **-ir** verbs have in common. This feature of the verb system occurs in other tenses as well, but since the imperfect is usually the first tense students learn after some struggle with the three conjugations of the present tense (and all their irregularities), this news usually comes as a relief. These two sets of endings for the three verb groups are shown below, using the usual model verbs **hablar**, **comer**, and **vivir**, which are always regular:

HABLAR		COMER		VIVIR	
hablaba	hablábamos	comía	comíamos	vivía	vivíamos
hablabas	hablábais	comías	comíais	vivías	vivíais
hablaba	hablaban	comía	comían	vivía	vivían

Thirdly, the imperfect is elegantly economical—it reduces what in English is a verb phrase (or periphrastic verb) into one single word. Take a look at the following examples:

Mientras **iba** a la playa, **llovía**.	While I **was going** to the beach, it **was raining**.
De niño, siempre **jugaba** en la arena.	As a child, I **used to play** in the sand all the time.
	As a child, I **would play** in the sand all the time.

As the examples above show, Spanish has a one-word tense to express what English requires more than one word to express. The name of the tense, rightly understood from its Latin root, even helps learners understand how actions in the past are viewed. When we use the imperfect, actions are viewed in the past as in progress, *not completely over*. Thus, actions expressed in the imperfect form a backdrop or background to other events, as will be seen when the imperfect and the preterite are used together.

As the examples above also show, the Spanish imperfect should be used whenever English employs the periphrastic constructions "*was/were* + verb in the *-ing* form" or "*used to* + infinitive."

A note about the dangers of the English modal verb *would* (used in the second translation of the second Spanish sentence in the examples above): the English modal, auxiliary, or helping verb *would* can be rendered in different ways in Spanish. Sometimes it can be translated into the imperfect subjunctive, to express, for instance, what one was hoping that someone else *would* do (as we will see in Chapter 8, on the sequence of tenses). At other times, it is a true conditional, expressing what *would* happen if something else were the case. However, whenever *would* is used as an equivalent of *used to* plus a verb, it *must* be rendered into Spanish using the imperfect.

Finally, the imperfect is delightful to most learners because the correspondence of the English periphrastic forms to the Spanish one-word imperfect tense is highly reliable—not foolproof, but highly reliable. Some of the pitfalls will be explained later, in Chapter 3, when we contrast the use of the imperfect and the preterite and show how they are used in common. (Perhaps a fifth reason could be thrown in for good measure: students almost always find the forms of the imperfect tense fun to pronounce. In particular, the forms for the **-er** and **-ir** verbs help reinforce the fact that vowels bearing an accent are to be stressed in pronunciation.)

There are verbal clues that help learners remember when to use the imperfect. In fact, due to their meaning, many expressions simply attract the use of the imperfect. The following are a few examples of such expressions. Once learners get the idea of the way the imperfect views action in the past as a progressive aspect, they usually can think of or recognize many, many more:

mientras*	*while*
siempre	*always*
a veces	*sometimes*
de vez en cuando	*once in a while*
pocas veces	*seldom*
muchas veces	*many times, often*
todos los veranos	*every summer*

*And **cuando**, when synonymous with **mientras**.

A few more specific observations will reinforce the general concept of the imperfect as a tense that portrays a past action as in progress. For instance, in order to tell the *time of day* (that is, clock time), the verb **ser** must be in the imperfect. Likewise, to express a person's *age* in the past, the imperfect of the verb **tener** must be used.

Eran las cinco de la tarde cuando...	*It **was** five in the afternoon when . . .*
Ella **tenía** cuatro años cuando...	*She **was** four years old when . . .*

The imperfect is not used to portray an action as beginning or ending. That is, it is not used when the point is to make note of the beginning or end point of a past action. It is used to bring to mind what *used to happen* (*habitual* or *repeated* action in the past), to show what *was* happening at a particular time, and to *describe* past states of being—physical, mental, or emotional. Note how the imperfect is confirmed as the proper tense to use in Spanish when the single English verb can be replaced by "*used to* + infinitive" or "*was/were* + verb in the *-ing* form."

En la década de los sesenta, el *twist* **era** popular.	*In the 1960s, the twist **was** popular.* *. . . the twist **used to be** popular.*
Juan siempre **trabajaba** en casa el verano pasado.	*John always **worked** at home last summer.* *John **was working** at home all the time . . .*
Mi hermana **estaba** contenta en Nueva York.	*My sister **was** happy in New York.* *My sister **used to be** happy . . .*

Typically, in combination with the preterite, the imperfect provides the temporal background for other actions that began or ended within a given time frame; it is the function of the imperfect to establish that time frame. The actions that happen on that temporal stage are expressed in the preterite. Finally, the preterite and imperfect cannot be used interchangeably without greatly altering the meaning of a sentence, even though the two sentences may often both be perfectly grammatical. This will be examined in greater detail in Chapter 3, which is dedicated to comparing these two tenses.

EJERCICIO
1·1

Match the English verb phrases on the left with the Spanish imperfect forms on the right. Since first- and third-person singular forms are identical and since the third-person forms (singular and plural) are used for more than one set of subjects each, some of the forms on the right will be used more than once.

1. she was writing	a. hablaban
2. we used to go	b. escuchaba
3. you (**Uds.**) used to travel	c. trabajaba
4. you (**tú**) were seeing	d. hablábamos
5. I used to make	e. corrían
6. he used to write	f. preguntaba
7. she was (**ser**)	g. buscábamos
8. they were traveling	h. comía
9. you (**Ud.**) used to be (**ser**)	i. escribía
10. you (**tú**) were looking for	j. era
11. I was eating	k. hacía
12. she was making	l. veías
13. we were going	m. trabajaban
14. we used to look for	n. íbamos
15. he used to eat	o. buscabas
16. I was asking	p. viajaban

17. they were running

18. we were talking

19. I was working

20. you (**Ud.**) used to listen

21. you (**Uds.**) used to run

22. they were talking

23. he used to work

24. he was listening

25. she was working

EJERCICIO
1·2

Fill in the blanks with the correct imperfect forms of the verbs in parentheses.

1. El coro _____ mientras los fieles comulgaban. (cantar)

2. El verano pasado, nosotros siempre _____ en ese restaurante. (comer)

3. Mientras yo _____, mi esposa _____. (dormir/leer)

4. Mi padre _____ mucho en esa época. (trabajar)

5. En la Segunda Guerra Mundial, su abuelo _____ soldado. (ser)

6. Durante mis años en la universidad, yo _____ todas las noches. (estudiar)

7. El poeta _____ cada noche hasta dormirse sobre el escritorio. (escribir)

8. Ella _____ a sus padres cada fin de semana. (visitar)

9. Los exploradores del siglo XVI siempre _____ a lugares exóticos. (ir)

10. Los babilonios _____ los astros todo el tiempo. (observar)

11. Romeo _____ un gran amor por Julieta. (sentir)

12. Aunque él _____ hacerlo, la idea no le _____.
(poder/agradar)

13. Aunque yo la _____ bien, no _____ con ella.
(conocer/salir)

14. Desde la ventana del tren, yo _____ las lejanas montañas. (ver)

15. Tú ya _____ la respuesta a esa pregunta en la clase ayer. (saber)

16. Anoche, mientras el ladrón _____ la puerta, el guardia lo
_____ en silencio. (abrir/esperar)

17. Mientras tú _____ las noticias, me _____
anonadado. (oír/mirar)

18. Ayer no _____ nadie en la biblioteca. (haber)

19. Einstein _____ mucho en la naturaleza del universo. (pensar)

20. Yo sé que mi mamá me _____ mucho en esos años. (querer)

Translate the following sentences from Spanish to English.

1. Los chicos no querían volver a casa porque se divertían mucho jugando al fútbol.

   _____

2. Los caballos galopaban por las pampas por varias horas en busca de agua.

   _____

3. ¿Cómo te sentías cuando tu hija iba a casarse?

   _____

4. Mientras yo escribía estos ejercicios, escuchaba música latina.

   _____

5. Yo surfeaba cada tarde por seis horas cuando vivía en Hawai.

_____

6. Para llegar a ser una pianista experta, ella practicaba todos los días.

_____

7. Mi esposa preparaba muchos platos típicos mientras trabajábamos en el jardín.

_____

8. El trabajo era muy duro y tomábamos mucha agua todo el día.

_____

9. Aunque lo agarraban siempre que cruzaba la frontera, volvía con las mismas ganas.

_____

10. Ese muchacho a veces me ganaba los partidos de ajedrez que jugábamos.

_____

11. Esa pareja antes bailaba toda la noche, pero ahora son un par de viejos enamorados.

_____

12. Poco a poco, íbamos penetrando en una región desconocida de la selva amazónica.

_____

13. La luna salía por el horizonte acuático a mi derecha mientras yo, a los 21° N., contemplaba la Osa Mayor.

_____

14. Cuando yo era niño, tenía la mala costumbre de echarle mucha sal a la comida.

_____

15. En la Edad de la Piedra, no había carros ni aviones.

_____

Translate the following sentences from English to Spanish.

1. While they were traveling through the desert, they observed the many varieties of cactus.

_____

2. It was around two in the morning and they were reading.

_____

3. Did you (**tú**) used to eat only vegetables when you lived in India?

_____

4. Her friends used to believe that she was able to dance well.

_____

5. We used to go to the movies nearly every night when we were living there.

_____

6. While we were flying, none of the flight attendants was able to rest.

_____

7. He was preparing the dinner and she was mixing the salad.

_____

8. Every time they would come to our house, we would play cards until midnight.

_____

9. There used to be no crime in this city.

_____

10. When they were fourteen or fifteen years old, they used to sleep on the beach.

_____

11. In the distance, I could hear the train that was traveling to Chicago.

_____

12. He was reading but they were writing.

    _____

13. He was famous.

    _____

14. There were five people in the restaurant last night at eleven o'clock.

    _____

15. Did they want to go with you?

    _____

The preterite

Narration, or what happened?

If learners of Spanish want to succeed in the long run, they must master the indicative forms of the present and preterite, for their own sakes and because the present and imperfect subjunctive forms are based, respectively, on these two tenses. This chapter will cover the preterite indicative for both regular and irregular verbs, as well as the uses of the preterite. In addition, we will make observations about four common verbs whose meanings in the preterite are different from their meanings in the present or imperfect.

After having invested time and effort to master the patterns and irregularities of the present tense, most learners experience some degree of frustration as they encounter a new set of problems in the preterite. Their consternation is understandable, since not only are they dealing with new paradigms, regular and irregular, but most of the verbs affected are the very same ones that were irregular in the present. The differences in pattern spell doom for learners who study haphazardly. They will confuse the types and patterns of irregularity and end up producing verb forms so bizarre that no native speaker of Spanish is likely to understand them. This chapter is designed to fix that problem or, if possible, to prevent it entirely.

Learners are encouraged to undertake a review of the present tense if they are unsure of its patterns, since this book on the past tenses assumes that they know the present well. Naturally, the book has been designed knowing that, if you are indeed at the critical crossroads just described, you are not alone in your frustration.

Regular verbs

First, let's examine the morphology of the preterite; that is, its verb endings. First we will look at the regular verbs, exemplified by **hablar**, **comer**, and **vivir**. The first thing that will particularly attract your attention is that as in the imperfect, there are two, not three, sets of endings. The regular -**ar** verbs have their own set of endings, while the regular -**er** and -**ir** verbs share one set of endings.

HABLAR		COMER		VIVIR	
hablé	hablamos	comí	comimos	viví	vivimos
hablaste	hablasteis	comiste	comisteis	viviste	vivisteis
habló	hablaron	comió	comieron	vivió	vivieron

In order to internalize these patterns and keep from confusing them with the present, it is good to seek patterns within the patterns and to contrast these with what happens in the present. First, observe that in the first- and third-person singular forms, in all cases, the stress falls on the last syllable. (Remember that we are talking about only *regular* verbs here.) The most common pitfall is to confuse **hablo** (present tense, *I speak*) with **habló** (preterite, *he* or *she speaks* or *you* [**Ud.**] *speak*), either by misusing the accent mark when writing or mispronouncing them.

Second, notice how the **nosotros** forms still end in **-mos** for all three conjugations. This is something that will happen throughout the entire verb system in every tense and mood, but what precedes the personal ending (including stem changes) is what identifies tense or mood. For the preterite of **-ar** and **-ir** verbs, there is no change from the present in their **nosotros** forms. Context will be the only means of knowing whether they mean *we speak* or *we spoke*, *we live* or *we lived*. For **-er** verbs, however, since they share the same endings as **-ir** verbs in the preterite but not in the present, there is a difference (**comemos** vs. **comimos**).

Seeking out constants in the verb system, we next discover that the third-person plural forms still end with an **-n**; moreover, we see that the new feature in the preterite is that all three third-person plural conjugations in the preterite now end in **-ron**. That leaves the vowels between the stem and the personal ending requiring close attention (**-a-** for **-ar** verbs; **-ie-** for **-er** and **-ir** verbs).

In the preterite, the **tú** and **vosotros** forms are so different from the **tú** and **vosotros** forms of all other tenses and moods that most learners find them easy to remember. As for the third-person singular forms, keep the stressed end vowel in mind and do *not* place the accent (in writing or in speaking) on the **-i-** of the **-er** and **-ir** forms. One way to avoid this is to remember that the stress falls on the final **-ó** for *all three* conjugations if the verb is *regular*.

Lastly, verbs whose infinitives end with **-car**, **-zar**, and **-gar** are often listed as irregular due to the spelling modification needed for the first-person singular only, in the preterite. Another way to look at these three groups of verbs is to remember that they are *regular in the way they sound*, but that Spanish orthography requires the spelling changes, as the following shows:

busqué	buscamos	empecé	empezamos	entregué	entregamos
buscaste	buscasteis	empezaste	empezasteis	entregaste	entregasteis
buscó	buscaron	empezó	empezaron	entregó	entregaron

Irregular verbs

Verbs that are irregular in the preterite are irregular in that they have new stems. Observe the preterite of the verb **tener**, the model for all verbs that have a new stem in the preterite. Note that regardless of whether an irregular verb ends in **-ar**, **-er**, or **-ir**, it shares this same set of endings. Also observe that, unlike in the regular verbs, the final vowel of the ending of the first- and third-person singular forms is *not* stressed:

tuve	tuvimos
tuviste	tuvisteis
tuvo	tuvieron

The common verb **dar** is conjugated as if it were a regular **-er** or **-ir** verb, but with no written accent on first- and third-person singular forms:

di	dimos
diste	disteis
dio	dieron

All of the irregular stems ending in **-j** omit the **-i-** of the third-person plural ending in the preterite. Other than that, they use the same pattern of endings as the rest of the irregular preterite verbs:

conduje	condujimos
condujiste	condujisteis
condujo	condujeron

Reviewing the peculiarities of the verbs that are irregular in the preterite, we find that (1) they all share one set of endings whether or not they are **-ar**, **-er**, or **-ir** verbs; (2) their first- and third-person singular endings are not stressed as are the endings of the regular verbs; and (3) the verbs whose new stems end in **-j** drop the **-i-** from the third-person plural ending.

Often, the new stems of the verbs that are irregular in the preterite bear so little resemblance to the stem of the present, or of the infinitive, that the best strategy for learning them (which, strangely enough, is not found in any Spanish textbook I have ever seen) is to memorize the **yo** form and **tú** form in the present, followed by the infinitive, then the **yo** form of the preterite. Following is a sampling of what learners should repeat and memorize when learning new verbs, in order to attain clarity and confidence in their knowledge of the Spanish verb system:

hablo, hablas; hablar; hablé
como, comes; comer; comí
vivo, vives; vivir; viví
conozco, conoces; conocer; conocí
pienso, piensas; pensar; pensé
puedo, puedes; poder; pude
tengo, tienes; tener; tuve
estoy, estás; estar; estuve
digo, dices; decir; dije
quiero, quieres; querer; quise
vengo, vienes; venir; vine
sé, sabes; saber; supe
traigo, traes; traer; traje
traduzco, traduces; traducir; traduje
ando, andas; andar; anduve

When you know the verb forms listed above, you can derive all the other verb forms from them. The beauty of this pedagogical method, in which the learner memorizes the present and the preterite (with the infinitive sandwiched in between), is that it works for both regular and irregular verbs, as learners will discover upon examining the present and preterite **yo** forms of various verbs in the paradigm.

Some learners may recognize that the method was derived by making a very slight modification of the *principal parts* method for learning Latin verbs (used by schoolboys in ancient Rome). Spanish, being a Romance language, responds very well to this system. It works for almost all Spanish verbs. The exceptions are **haber**, **ir**, **saber**, and **ser**, whose conjugations are best dealt with by memorizing their present subjunctive forms because, unlike with other verbs, their present subjunctive forms do not fit any pattern established by their present indicatives (e.g., there is nothing in the form **sé** that suggests that **sepa** is the **yo**—and also the third-person singular—form of the present subjunctive. But for all other Spanish verbs, by memorizing the verbs as vocabulary items in the manner outlined above, learners can foreground in their memory the principal patterns for deriving *all* the forms for all the indicative *and* subjunctive forms, in both the present and preterite, whether the pattern is regular or not!

In the preterite, one does not find the *shoe* or *boot* pattern of vowel stem changes found in the present, when the verb is conjugated in a grid consisting of three rows indicating first-, second- and third-person and two columns, the left-hand one for the singular and the right-hand one for the plural forms. A common and dangerous error that learners make is to transfer the irregular pattern of one tense to another tense that does not actually share that pattern. Still, there are a handful of verbs that do have a stem-vowel irregularity in the preterite. They are **servir**, **pedir**, **repetir**, **morir**, and **dormir**. In the present and preterite, the stem vowel -**e**- in **servir**, **pedir**, and **repetir** changes to -**i**-. In **morir** and

The preterite   **13**

dormir, the **-o-** changes to **-ue-** in the present but only to **-u-** in the preterite. In the present, these changes occur in the shoe pattern, but in the preterite, these changes occur only in the third-person, singular and plural, as seen below:

PRESENT: SHOE PATTERN		PRETERITE: THIRD-PERSON FORMS ONLY	
sirvo	servimos	serví	servimos
sirves	servís	serviste	servisteis
sirve	sirven	sirvió	sirvieron

PRESENT: SHOE PATTERN		PRETERITE: THIRD-PERSON FORMS ONLY	
duermo	dormimos	dormí	dormimos
duermes	dormís	dormiste	dormisteis
duerme	duermen	durmió	durmieron

Uses of the preterite

In terms of usage, the preterite is a tense that narrates past actions in the past and views them as completed, over, done with. Julius Caesar's famous line *veni, vidi, vici* (*I came, I saw, I conquered*) were the Latin forms of what became the preterite of Spanish. Since the preterite expresses actions as completed, if the beginning or end of an action is stated, or some temporal beginning or end point is mentioned, only the preterite may be used. Consider the following example:

Estuve en la biblioteca hasta las tres.   *I **was** in the library until three o'clock.*

Since *three o'clock* is mentioned explicitly, the imperfect (**estaba**) is not admissible in this sentence. If three o'clock had not been mentioned, but rather some vague notion of the past, such as **ayer** (*yesterday*), then either the preterite or the imperfect could have been used. The differences of meaning that result from a choice between these two tenses will be taken up in the following chapter.

There are four verbs in Spanish that change their meaning when used in the preterite. They are **querer**, **poder**, **saber**, and **conocer**. Another way to look at this situation is to remember that if the primary meaning of any of these verbs is needed in a past tense, then the imperfect, not the preterite, must be used. (The contrast between the two tenses will be discussed in more detail in the next chapter.) The preterite meaning of each of these verbs is shown in the following examples. Note what happens, in particular, to **querer** and **poder** when they are used in an affirmative or negative sense. The first-person singular of each of these verbs is shown here for the sake of brevity:

Quise abrir la ventana.   *I **tried** to open the window.*
No quise abrir la ventana.   *I **refused** to open the window.*

Pude abrir la ventana.	I **succeeded** in opening the window.
	I **managed** to get the window open.
No pude abrir la ventana.	I **failed** to open the window.
	I **couldn't** get the window open.

Anoche, **supe** que Juan está en el hospital.	Last night, I **found out** that John is in the hospital.
No **supe** que Juan está en el hospital hasta anoche.	I **didn't find out** that John is in the hospital until last night.

Conocí a María en la fiesta.	I **met** Maria at the party.
No conocí a María en la fiesta, sino en el parque.	I **didn't meet** Maria at the party, but rather in the park.

In the following exercises, only the preterite will be called for. This is because of the need to reinforce the many irregular stems that must be memorized in order to manage this tense with confidence.

EJERCICIO
2·1

Match the English verb phrases on the left with the Spanish preterite forms on the right. Since the third-person forms, singular and plural, can refer to what are six different subjects in English, some of the forms on the right will be used more than once.

1. they wrote	a. di
2. she did	b. dijo
3. you (**Ud.**) made	c. conduje
4. they came	d. pusiste
5. he made	e. no quiso
6. I succeeded	f. vio
7. we were (**estar**)	g. hablé
8. I brought	h. pidieron
9. he and she served	i. vivió
10. you (**tú**) said	j. fui
11. they were (**ser**)	k. tradujeron

12. she and I had	l.	fueron
13. you (**vosotros**) ate	m.	dijiste
14. you (**Uds.**) translated	n.	tuvimos
15. he lived	o.	comisteis
16. they ordered	p.	estuvimos
17. you (**Uds.**) were (**ser**)	q.	traje
18. I went	r.	sirvieron
19. she refused	s.	vinieron
20. I spoke	t.	pude
21. he saw	u.	hizo
22. you (**tú**) put	v.	escribieron
23. she said		
24. I gave		
25. I drove		

EJERCICIO
2·2

Fill in the blanks with the correct preterite forms of the verbs in parentheses.

1. ¿Qué le _____ tú a la señora en la tienda ayer? (decir)

2. Yo no la _____ en la fiesta anoche. (conocer)

3. Ella no _____ la suerte de Juana quien ganó la lotería el año pasado. (tener)

4. Anoche, él _____ que su equipo favorito ahora es el número uno en el país. (saber)

5. Yo _____ la cuenta anoche en el restaurante y salí en seguida. (pagar)

6. La niña _____ el cuento en media hora. (leer)

7. Juana no _____ salir con él porque ese chico no tiene buenos modales. (querer)

8. Tú nos _____ un regalo cómico el Día de las Mentiras. (dar)

9. Tomás y yo _____ demasiado pastel después de la cena. (comer)

10. ¿No _____ tú el partido en la tele anoche? ¡Fue un espectáculo! (ver)

11. Después de varias horas de trabajo, Juan _____ sacar la piedra del jardín. (poder)

12. Julio César _____ un gran general romano. (ser)

13. Cuando empezó esa clase, yo _____ a roncar. (comenzar)

14. Setenta y dos traductores _____ la Septuaginta. (traducir)

15. Esa chica es inteligente; ¡Juan no _____ convencerla a salir con él! (poder)

16. Todos nosotros _____ algo al picnic. (traer)

17. Luciano _____ varios años en EE.UU. antes de morir. (cantar)

18. Mamá, ¿dónde _____ mi camisa de seda? (poner)

19. Él _____ invitarla a la fiesta, pero ella no _____ salir con él. (querer/querer)

20. ¿No _____ tú a la playa la semana pasada? Perdiste un día muy agradable. (ir)

21. Ellos _____ allí tomando el sol por un par de horas. (estar)

22. Ud. _____ a EE.UU. hace un año para trabajar en esta compañía, ¿no? (venir)

23. Yo _____ el guante en el teatro por media hora y no lo encontré. (buscar)

24. Ellos _____ en San Juan por cinco años. (vivir)

25. Uds. _____ toda la noche sobre sus aventuras en Madrid. (hablar)

Translate the following sentences from Spanish to English.

1. La leche se estropeó después de tantos días en la refrigeradora.

   _____

2. Las tropas entregaron las armas después de perder la batalla.

   _____

3. Los peces tropicales murieron de una intoxicación de cobre en el tanque.

   _____

4. No quise estudiar química en la escuela.

   _____

5. Sus padres insistieron en ir a ver el drama de Navidad con los vecinos.

   _____

6. La acompañaste hasta su casa, ¿no?

   _____

7. La madre defendió a su hijo.

   _____

8. Ellas le pidieron un pastel al mesero.

   _____

9. Mis amigos decidieron abrir una cuenta bancaria en Suiza.

   _____

10. ¿Buscaste el perro por cuántas horas anoche?

    _____

11. Le pegó un rayo, provocando un incendio que consumió todo el edificio.

    _____

12. Él se durmió en clase.

    _____

13. ¿A quién le diste los pendientes? ¿A María o a Cristina?

_____

14. Lo metieron en la cárcel por desfalco de fondos.

_____

15. Empecé a cantar y mis amigos se taparon los oídos.

_____

16. Tuvimos un examen en la clase de geometría esta mañana.

_____

17. La niña apenas se cayó del columpio hace un minuto.

_____

18. Conocí a mi esposa en 1990.

_____

19. Ellos condujeron a San Diego, tomando turnos de seis horas por tres días seguidos.

_____

20. ¿Quién me trajo este sombrero?

_____

Translate the following sentences from English to Spanish.

1. We went to Vegas last month.

_____

2. She and Teresa translated this article.

_____

3. I found out that she is honest when she told me the truth about her brother.

_____

4. Did you (**tú**) try to open the door?

_____

5. He and I came home very late last night.

_____

6. I looked for them for an hour.

_____

7. She failed to start the car.

_____

8. Did you (**tú**) and John go to the cafeteria this morning?

_____

9. She met her present (**actual**) husband at Juanita's party last December.

_____

10. They broke the window.

_____

11. The waitress served us the **sangría** and **tapas**.

_____

12. We couldn't find the suitcase.

_____

13. I paid the cabbie and went to my hotel room.

_____

14. They tried to find us.

_____

15. It started to rain as soon as the game began.

_____

16. She and I met him at the soccer game.

_____

17. We refused to buy the car.

_____

18. They tried to climb the mountain.

_____

19. He saw the movie three times.

_____

20. They climbed the steps to the cathedral.

_____

·3· The imperfect and the preterite together

Narrating and describing in the past

Mastery of the use of the preterite and the imperfect together is one of the first big hurdles for learners of Spanish. In a few hours they can be secure with the forms of the imperfect. In weeks, or possibly months, they can feel secure about the forms of the preterite. By the time the forms of these two tenses are mastered, they also should understand and appreciate them as two aspects of the past that are not interchangeable. Yet, as all learners and their teachers know from experience, it is one thing to understand the concept and another to remember the details in the nick of time, especially when speaking.

This chapter will put learners on the right path to making the proper choice in each case and to gaining the confidence that they are using them correctly. It is likely that for some time, learners will remember the right thing to say—after they have made an error. This too is normal. In fact, self-correction is an indication of emerging proficiency and should be regarded as encouragement to continue studying.

In the previous two chapters, the ways in which the preterite and the imperfect view past action were examined separately. As was mentioned in those chapters, the preterite and the imperfect are often used together. Learners can now begin to appreciate the richness of expression that derives from their being used in tandem.

To review briefly, the preterite views an action in the past as completed, or focuses on its beginning or end. By contrast, the imperfect views actions in the past as a process whose beginning or end is not of interest. This makes their combined use so expressively rich that the best word to describe their reciprocal effect is cinematographic—they create vivid moving images in the minds of listeners and speakers. The imperfect, with its focus on past actions as *in progress*, expresses most clearly and unmistakably what the background or circumstance is in which other actions occurred. The function of the preterite is to relate the actions that occurred in that circumstance. In the following two renditions of the same basic sentence, note that it does not matter which tense comes first. Note that **cuando** (*when*) has the same meaning as **mientras** (*while*), in both Spanish and English, when the imperfect is used.

Los soldados **no atacaron** cuando la luna **estaba** llena.	*The soldiers **did not attack** when the moon **was full**.*
Cuando la luna **estaba** llena, los soldados **no atacaron**.	*When the moon **was full**, the soldiers **did not attack**.*

Of course, it is always possible to use the imperfect to indicate the simultaneity of two actions, processes or circumstances in the past. Observe below how the meaning of the above sentences changes radically when both verbs are in the imperfect. Note too the various ways that English has for dealing with what the Spanish imperfect conveys so economically with one word:

Los soldados **atacaban** cuando la luna **estaba** llena.	*The soldiers **were attacking** when the moon **was full**.*
	*The soldiers **used to attack** whenever the moon **was full**.*
	*The soldiers **usually attacked** while there **was** a full moon.*
	*The soldiers **would attack** when the moon **was full**.*

As the last example above reveals, when both verbs are in the imperfect, the imperfect also has the function of telling what actions happened habitually or repeatedly in the past. The sentence is a likely one if found in a description of some army's tactical operations.

Examining this more closely, in the sentence in which the preterite and the imperfect are used together, however, the preterite (**no atacaron**) can refer only to one particular night of the month, during which the moon was full. In either case, however, only the imperfect can be used when describing the full moon because the moon cannot suddenly become full. Since the moon's changes from phase to phase involve a process that is continuous and ongoing, describing a past situation in which the moon was in this or that phase makes this natural phenomenon an ideal way to convey an understanding of the imperfect and leads to a more certain mastery of the use of these two past tenses together.

Let's examine two more pairs of sentences, each pair being rendered once with the preterite and the imperfect contrasted, and then with both verbs in the imperfect. It is easy to see how what one means to say determines the choice:

El barco **se hundió** cuando **llegaba** al puerto.	*The ship **sank** when it **was arriving** in port.*
El barco **se hundía** cuando **llegaba** al puerto.	*The ship **was sinking** while it **was coming** into port.*
La casa **estaba quemándose** cuando yo **llegué**.	*The house **was burning** when I **arrived**.*

La casa **estaba quemándose** cuando yo **llegaba**.	*The house **was burning** while I **was arriving**.* *The house **was burning** while I **was on my way** there.*

The preterite is the only proper choice of past tense whenever a speaker is faced with narrating a series of sequenced past actions. The famous line of Caesar when he returned from the conquest of Bithynia in Asia Minor, already mentioned in Chapter 2—*veni, vidi, vici*—is the classic example of this. The pithy phrase translates as *I came, I saw, I conquered*, showing that these actions happened *in just that order* and thus rhetorically informed his listeners that the whole matter of the Bithynian campaign was over and done.

Los niños **se levantaron, se bañaron, se vistieron** y **salieron** corriendo al patio.	*The children **got up, bathed, got dressed**, and **went** running out to the patio.*
Su padre **tomó** la iniciativa: **vendió** la casa y **se mudaron** a la Patagonia.	*His father **took** the initiative: he **sold** the house and they **moved** to Patagonia.*

Sometimes it is pointed out that the preterite is often the right choice when the English uses a simple (one-word) form in the past. This rule of thumb is not fail-safe because it can fail to take into account the *meaning* in English. Therefore, to refine that rule and make it far more reliable, keep this in mind: If the meaning of the one-word English form remains unchanged when replaced by the English verb phrase "*used to* + infinitive," "*was/were* + verb in *-ing*," or "*would* + infinitive," the imperfect aspect is being expressed in English and must be translated by the imperfect in Spanish. Examine the following examples (noting that the direction is from English into Spanish, the direction which causes the confusion, of course, for English-speaking learners of Spanish):

*While the boss **spoke**, we **looked** around the room.*	Mientras **hablaba** el jefe, **mirábamos** por la sala.
*She **cooked** for them when they **lived** here.*	Ella les **preparaba** la comida cuando **vivían** aquí.

In the following example, notice how the use of the English one-word past form can result in ambiguity, particularly if no context is provided or already understood:

When they ran down the hill, they could see the beach.

The speaker of the above sentence could mean to communicate any of the following scenarios:

That time they ran down the hill, they arrived at a point where they saw the beach.
All the while that they were running down the hill, they were able to see the beach.

Depending on the terrain in question, the sentence could even mean:

> *When they started running down the hill, the beach was still visible* (but not from farther down the hill).

In Spanish, the proper choice of the past tenses will eliminate these ambiguities. In order to begin to translate the original English sentence, contexts have to be guessed at, giving three possible interpretations, as follows:

Cuando **bajaron** la colina, **pudieron ver** la playa.	*Once they **got to the bottom** of the hill, they **managed to see** the beach.*
Mientras **bajaban** la colina, **podían ver** la playa.	*While they **were going down** the hill, they **were able to view** the beach.*
Cuando **se echaron a bajar** la colina, **se veía** la playa todavía.	*When they **started down** the hill, the beach **could** still **be seen**.*

Notice that the English translations above are translations of the various conceptual interpretations of the original ambiguous sentence. This is a short lesson in how the original English sentence might have been improved so as to eliminate the ambiguity and suggests the uniquely human quality of language.

Ser versus estar

One of the most challenging situations for English-speaking learners of Spanish is when they are faced with *was* or *were* in English. The problem is compounded by the need to decide which of the two possible Spanish verbs to use as well as whether to use the preterite or the imperfect. Yet there is a simple decision tree that learners can use to greatly reduce their errors when making the choice between the preterite and the imperfect in Spanish.

Remember that **ser** is the *be* verb used for expressing identity, possession, origin, and material composition as well as, with adjectives, the normative or characteristic features of a noun. **Estar**, on the other hand, the other *be* verb, is used for expressing health and location as well as, with adjectives, for describing a noun with respect to some change of condition. Remember too that, depending on the use of **ser** or **estar**, an adjective often expresses a different idea. Observe the following examples:

Ser

Es un hombre.	*It's a man.*
Ese hombre **es** alto.	*That man **is** tall.*
Ese hombre **es** José.	*That man **is** José.*
José **es** de México.	*José **is** from Mexico.*
José **es** de carne y hueso.	*José **is** made of flesh and blood.*
José **es** enfermo.	*José **is** sickly.*

Estar

José **está** aquí.	*José **is** here.*
José **está** bien.	*José **is** fine.*
José **está** enfermo.	*José **is** ill.*

In the past tenses, the uses of these two verbs are just as strictly observed, but since both the preterite and the imperfect are one-word forms, the decision of whether to use the preterite or the imperfect can be perplexing. Interestingly, one can *almost always* use the imperfect of **estar** and avoid the preterite. This one omission from one's usual repertoire simplifies the learner's task, because the resulting three choices for any given person and number means that the first question one needs to resolve is whether **ser** or **estar** is needed—a question usually reducible to whether one is dealing with health or location.

Then, if **estar** is needed, the decision is made and the imperfect can be used with confidence. The only time the preterite of **estar** is required is when a specific past time is mentioned. Remembering that the preterite is used whenever the beginning or end point of an action is implied or stated will help learners avoid making an error in those few occasions.

Oye, Juan, ¿dónde **estabas** ayer?	*Say, John, where **were** you yesterday?*
Oye, Juan, ¿dónde **estuviste** a las tres?	*Say, John, where **were** you at three?*

Next, notice that the first example below, like the second example above, makes explicit reference to either a specific time or a clearly demarcated period. The second two examples below are more interesting and show that if a speaker wishes to use a time frame in a very literal way (**semana** being a seven-day period), the use of the preterite shows, in the first example, that the speaker's sister was sick for the whole period. On the other hand, if **semana** is meant to be not specific but rather a general time frame, during some part of which the speaker's sister was sick, then the imperfect is used:

Mi hermana **estuvo** enferma por un día.	*My sister **was** sick for a day.*
Mi hermana **estuvo** enferma esa semana.	*My sister **was** sick all that week.*
Mi hermana **estaba** enferma esa semana.	*My sister **was** sick during part of that week.*

Finally, if it is **ser** that is needed, there remains only the question of whether to use the preterite or imperfect of this verb. Reducing that problem is not difficult. If **ser** is needed to summarize something, as if it were *closing a door* on a matter (*period*, full stop!), the preterite will be used. If it appears to be inviting elaboration, the imperfect *opens the door* to more information:

Simón Bolívar **fue** el George Washington de Latinoamérica.	*Simón Bolívar **was** the George Washington of Latin America.*

Simón Bolívar **era** un hombre muy famoso del siglo XIX. Liberó...	*Simón Bolívar **was** a famous figure of the nineteenth century. He liberated . . .*

In my introduction to the two examples above, I used the metaphor of closing or opening a door. Another way of looking at the difference between the preterite and the imperfect is cinematographically: the imperfect is often compared to a camera as it pans a scene, acting as someone's memory—but a scene in which nothing is happening, yet. The description of such a scene in the past requires the use of the imperfect. Any action or actions that happen in this flashback would be, if put into words, in the preterite. Another analogy, also from the movies, is that if it is dealing with an action and not just a static scene, the imperfect is like a slow-motion camera that catches an action in the middle of things, since it focuses on the process, not the beginning or end of an action. Examine these sentences in which the two tenses are used together:

Era una noche oscura y **llovía** cuando el asesino **llegó** a la oficina.	*It **was** a dark night and it **was raining** when the murderer **arrived** at the office.*
El asesino **abría** la puerta lentamente para no hacer ruido, pero el perro lo **olfateó**.	*The murderer **was opening** the door slowly so as to make no noise, but the dog **smelled** him.*

Indeed, the famously clichéd horror-story beginning *It was a dark and stormy night* places the reader or viewer in the midst of the situation. Likewise, in the second example above, the slow opening of the door is in progress when the moviegoer's eye or the reader's mind's eye is treated to the opening scene. Despite being actions, they are presented as in progress. They are *descriptive*. They do not advance the plot. The imperfect is the tense used to present past actions in this descriptive way.

Note how the other actions in the examples above advance the story. They move it forward, and are said to be *narrative*. The murderer *arrived*. The dog *smelled* the murderer. Once done, these actions cannot be undone. The expression of actions in this manner is the function of the preterite.

Poder, querer, saber, and conocer

Once learners have a good grasp of the way in which these two tenses view time, that is, of their being two aspects of the past, they can more easily appreciate how four verbs, when used in the preterite, do not mean the same thing as their first, standard dictionary meanings. It may be more useful to look at this from the point of view of an English speaker who has something to say in Spanish, and to restate the observation: there are several past forms of English verbs whose meanings in Spanish are found in four verbs, and these meanings are only obtained by using those verbs in the preterite. These four verbs, with their standard meanings in parentheses, are: **poder** (*to be able*), **querer** (*to want*), **saber** (*to know*—facts, information), and **conocer** (*to know* people or *be acquainted with something*).

Since the preterite is used to depict actions either as completed (compressing time) or as beginning or ending, these four verbs simply cannot mean the same thing in the preterite. Thus, we can now learn which English verbs in the past correspond in meaning to the preterite forms of these four Spanish verbs. Note that there are different English verbs corresponding to the affirmative and negative uses of **poder** and **querer** in the preterite:

Poder

Juan **pudo** escalar la montaña.	*Juan **succeeded** at climbing the mountain.*
Juan **no pudo** hacer el ejercicio.	*Juan **failed** to do the exercise.*

Querer

Juana **quiso** abrir la ventana.	*Juana **tried** to open the window.*
Juana **no quiso** salir con Enrique.	*Juana **refused** to go out with Enrique.*

Saber

Lo **supe** cuando llegué a casa.	*I **found** it **out** when I arrived home.*
No lo **supieron** hasta que se lo dije.	*They **didn't find** it **out** until I told them.*

Conocer

Juan **conoció** a María en la fiesta.	*John **met** Maria at the party.*
Yo nunca la **conocí**.	*I never **met** her.*

Another rule that reflects the imperfective nature of certain types of actions is that when telling time in the past or speaking of age in the past, the imperfect is nearly always the only possible tense to use (unless the speaker is summarizing or condensing time, as in the third example below). Just as the moon's phases are a process and the moon does not suddenly become full, quarter, or half, time and age (really the same thing, after all) are phenomena that involve the smooth onward-moving flow of time:

Yo **tenía** cinco años cuando **aprendí** a montar en bicicleta.	*I **was** five when I **learned** to ride a bicycle.*
Eran las cinco cuando el barco **llegó**.	*It **was** five when the boat **came in**.*
Yo **tuve** quince años **una vez** y comprendo lo que te sientes.	*I **was** fifteen **once** and understand how you feel.*

There is one use of the imperfect that will be taken up in Chapter 6, on the conditional: the use of the imperfect in indirect statements. The imperfect's use is identical in meaning to one of the two ways in which the conditional can be used in an indirect statement.

Preterite or imperfect? Fill in the blanks with the proper forms of the verbs in parentheses.

1. Mientras _____ anoche, yo dormía en el sofá. (llover)

2. Después de estudiar, mi amigo _____ cinco millas. (correr)

3. Juan le _____ una carta y yo estudiaba. (escribir)

4. ¿Qué _____ tú después de ver la película? (hacer)

5. Ella lo _____ aunque nadie creía que volviera. (esperar)

6. ¿Dónde estabas cuando _____ sobre el accidente? (saber)

7. Para concluir, es obvio que John Lennon _____ un músico talentoso. (ser)

8. Aunque intentó varias veces, nunca _____ escalar esa montaña. (poder)

9. Cuando Caperucita Roja _____ por el bosque, recogía flores. (ir)

10. Aunque yo lo _____ hacer, nunca tenía suficientes ganas de hacerlo. (poder)

11. Nosotros lo buscábamos toda la tarde, pero no _____ por aquí. (estar)

12. Fidel _____ por siete horas. (hablar)

13. Nosotros tuvimos hambre, así que _____ al Plato de Oro. (ir)

14. Tras varios años de noviazgo, Amaranta _____ no casarse con Crespi. (decidir)

15. Durante el viaje en tren, ellos _____ por la ventana al desierto que parecía no tener límites. (mirar)

16. De repente, mis amigos _____ una orca. (ver)

17. Juanito, ¿qué te _____ la maestra sobre lo que hiciste la semana pasada? (decir)

18. Aquéllos _____ días difíciles, pues no sabíamos si íbamos a vivir o morir. (ser)

19. El chico _____ salir con María una vez aunque el padre de ella lo odiaba. (querer)

20. Ella _____ el libro en la silla porque no quería que nadie se sentara en ella. (poner)

21. Los padres de Susana siempre le _____ que saliera con muchachos. (prohibir)

22. Yo _____ deprimido aun antes de saber las noticias. (sentirse)

23. Él _____ la caja con cuidado, temiendo una revancha de las maldiciones de Pandora. (abrir)

24. Cantó el gallo y nos _____ . (despertar)

25. Juan, ¿no la _____ cuando estabas de vacaciones? (conocer)

Fill in the blanks with the proper forms of the verbs in parentheses, using either the preterite or the imperfect in the most logical way.

1. Desde San Francisco a Portland en tren, yo _____ una novela,

   pero tú _____ el paisaje por la ventana. (leer/mirar)

2. El veterinario _____ el perro y _____ que no tenía nada grave. (examinar/concluir)

3. Yo la _____ a salir conmigo pero ella no _____ acompañarme. (invitar/querer)

4. Juan _____ todo el día y luego _____ toda la noche. (trabajar/descansar)

5. Aunque ellas _____ alcanzar la meta ese día, no la

   _____ . (intentar/lograr)

6. Las chicas _____ y _____ todas las noches en el club. (cantar/bailar)

7. _____ obvio que Juan _____ celoso. (ser/estar)

8. Mis amigos _____ asistir a la reunión, pero por las

   circunstancias no _____ . (querer/poder)

9. Mientras mi mamá _____ el pastel, tú _____
   la ensalada. (hacer/preparar)

10. El sábado pasado, el alpinista _____ subir el Everest, pero a

    causa del frío, no _____ . (querer/poder)

11. Al paso que la secretaria _____ el informe, lo _____
    en su cuaderno. (escuchar/apuntar)

12. Teresa y Marta siempre _____ ropa en esa tienda pero nunca

    la _____ . (comprar/llevar)

13. Tú _____ a María cuando tú _____ por el
    parque ayer por la tarde. (ver/correr)

14. Cuando mi hermana _____ a la escuela ayer no se

    _____ el parque a causa de la niebla. (ir/ver)

15. Después de que _____ , Juan _____ al béisbol
    por un par de horas. (llover/jugar)

16. Tomás no lo _____ hasta que lo _____ con
    sus propios ojos. (creer/ver)

17. Las niñas _____ por el bosque y _____ flores
    al lado del sendero. (caminar/recoger)

18. Los tres cochinitos _____ las casas pero luego no las

    _____ . (construir/vender)

19. La joven _____ ir a la fiesta pero sus padres dijeron que

    no _____ . (desear/poder)

20. Cristóbal Colón _____ desde España hasta que

    _____ a las Américas. (navegar/llegar)

21. Ayer (yo) _____ a las siete y _____ en
    seguida. (despertarse/levantarse)

22. El anciano _____ la puerta y _____ las luces.
    (abrir/encender)

23. La semana pasada, nosotros _____ la lección y _____ que la luna no es de queso. (leer/saber)

24. Tú _____ la ventana pero no _____ la lámpara. (cerrar/apagar)

25. _____ el telón y la orquesta _____ a tocar. (subir/empezar)

26. Tan pronto como ella lo _____ , _____ de él. (ver/enamorarse)

EJERCICIO
3·3

Translate the following sentences from Spanish to English.

1. Los obreros abrieron el puente tan pronto como llegó el barco.

   _____

2. Mis amigos comían pizza pero yo prefería estudiar.

   _____

3. Su novia decidió romper con él porque no le gustaban sus cigarillos.

   _____

4. Mientras íbamos al banco, supimos por la radio que alguien estaba robándolo.

   _____

5. Los fanáticos futbolistas quisieron entrar en el estadio, pero los guardias no los dejaron pasar.

   _____

   _____

6. ¿No pudiste terminar la tarea? ¿Qué pasa? Es que no quisiste estudiar, ¿no?

   _____

7. Pasaron varias semanas y por fin ella le contestó con una larga carta, explicándole que no quería casarse con él sino con otro.

   _____

   _____

8. Mientras los niños jugaban en el jardín, su madre subió a la recámara para intentar dormir, pero no pudo.

   _____

   _____

9. Los bomberos llegaron al incendio y lo apagaron pronto.

   _____

10. Mientras volábamos de Madrid a Nueva York, miramos una película.

    _____

11. Los niños se vistieron, salieron a jugar y sólo regresaron cuando se ponía el sol.

    _____

12. Era un día fantástico: no hacía calor ni frío, no estaba nublado y yo no tenía nada que hacer.

    _____

    _____

13. Cuando Juan tenía ocho años, su familia se mudó del D.F. a San Antonio.

    _____

14. Los caminos estuvieron cerrados por varios días, y cuando los abrieron, nadie pudo manejar en ellos a causa de los árboles caídos.

    _____

    _____

15. En el momento en que sus padres entraron, su novio saltó por la ventana y se fue.

    _____

16. Cada trueno hacía reverberar las ventanas; se sentía el frío entrar por debajo de las puertas cuando, de repente, la puerta pareció abrirse sola y entró una figura oscura.

    _____

    _____

17. Eran las cuatro cuando salimos del trabajo, pero no pudimos llegar a casa hasta las nueve a causa del tráfico.

    _____

    _____

18. El submarino descendió hasta que llegó a 2.000 pies bajo el nivel del mar, luego se quedó inmóvil por varias horas.

    _____

    _____

19. Los políticos hablaban por horas y, como siempre, nadie les creía.

    _____

20. En la fiesta anoche, las chicas empezaron a bailar pero los chicos seguían comiendo.

    _____

21. ¿Cuántos años tenías cuando tus padres te dieron permiso de salir solo al cine?

    _____

22. El perro dormía cuando el gato se comió toda su comida.

    _____

23. Cuando me desperté, el desayuno ya estaba listo.

    _____

24. Podíamos oler el café cuando entramos en el restaurante.

    _____

25. Cuando llegó mi padre, eran las ocho de la noche.

    _____

26. Había mucha gente que quería asistir al concierto pero muchos no pudieron porque no había suficientes asientos.

_____

_____

_____

Translate the following sentences from English to Spanish.

1. Where were your friends when you (**tú**) got home last night?

_____

2. The driver was sleeping when he lost control of the car.

_____

3. What time was it when you (**tú**) came to my house?

_____

4. Was she going to the party when it started to rain?

_____

5. You (**tú**) finished the novel after I arrived.

_____

6. The children did not know how to dress themselves.

_____

7. What did you (**tú**) do last weekend?

_____

8. When she learned what was happening at school, she called her friends.

_____

9. Did you (**tú**) try to meet him when he came to visit us?

_____

10. It was snowing last week but it was not very cold.

_____

11. They learned to read when they were seven years old.

_____

12. She was twenty-seven years old when we met.

_____

13. She put on her coat and left the house, even though it was raining.

_____

14. He tried to sell the house, but couldn't.

_____

15. I refused to leave my dog alone when I went on vacation last month.

_____

16. She met me at the university last year.

_____

17. They always went shopping together, but they never bought anything.

_____

18. I wanted to see the movie, but I couldn't make it.

_____

19. She tried to go to class, but couldn't make it.

_____

20. They wanted to go to the zoo, but they had to stay home.

_____

21. My family used to go to the beach on weekends.

_____

22. When he learned that she had gone out with his best friend, he refused to believe it.

_____

23. They were watching TV when the lights went out.

_____

24. He and I used to cook a lot.

_____

25. Teresa and Martha wanted to call me, but their phone was not working.

_____

26. My friend's mother was talking on the phone when I tried to call him.

_____

EJERCICIO
3·5

Fill in the blanks in the paragraphs below with the proper forms of the verbs in the list above each paragraph, in either the preterite or the imperfect. Be sure to read the paragraph well before you make any choices. Some verbs will be used more than once.

aprender	encontrar	pensar	creer	haber
saber	descubrir	morir	ser	

A. Durante el siglo XV, muchos (1) _____ que sólo

(2) _____ tres continentes: Europa, África y Asia. No

(3) _____ nadie de la existencia de los dos grandes continentes de

las Américas. ¡Aun Cristóbal Colón, quien "(4) _____" el "Nuevo

Mundo", (5) _____, hasta que (6) _____, que lo

que él (7) _____ (8) _____ parte de Asia! Después

de que él (9) _____, poco a poco los europeos

(10) _____ más sobre este hemisferio. ¡ (11) _____

una época de maravillas!

The imperfect and the preterite together   **37**

estar	jugar	querer	gustar	oír	saber
haber	llegar	ser	hacer	poder	ver
ir	preferir	volver			

B. Los tres amigos (1) _____ por la calle como les (2) _____

hacer siempre los días frescos de otoño cuando (3) _____ buen

tiempo. Ellos (4) _____ jugar al fútbol pero no (5) _____

si todos sus amigos (6) _____ a venir o no. Cuando

(7) _____ a la cancha donde generalmente (8) _____

los sábados, ellos (9) _____ que (10) _____ doce

compañeros de clase, listos para jugar. Desafortunadamente, después de hablar con

uno de ellos, (11) _____ que su amigo Jorge no (12) _____

jugar ese día porque (13) _____ enfermo. Cuando otros lo

(14) _____, no (15) _____ jugar sin él y muchos

(16) _____ volver a casa. (17) _____ las cinco

cuando por fin (18) _____ a casa.

The present perfect

What have you done for me lately?

4

Conversations I have had with professors who have observed the linguistic habits of students over the past twenty-five years have led me to suspect that the use of the present perfect in American English has been in slight decline over this period. Our collective anecdotal data suggest that the awareness of why the present perfect is not only useful but needful seems to be eluding many college students today.

The present perfect is necessary and always has been. The degree of precision that it gives to the information one communicates can be found by considering two answers to the common question: "Are you hungry?" The following two replies to that question exemplify how much richer one's communication can be and should be, not in stylistic terms, but in concrete informational ones, when using the second reply, an example of the present perfect tense in Spanish and English:

Ya **comí**, gracias.	I *ate*, *thanks.*
He comido, gracias.	I *have eaten, thanks.*

Take a look at the verb phrase in the second reply. It consists of the verb *have*, used in its capacity of a *helping*, or *auxiliary verb*, plus the past participle (or, as it is sometimes called, the *passive* participle). In most spoken English, the tendency to contract the helping verb into the subject pronoun, by saying *I've eaten, thanks*, is probably what partially obscures people's awareness of this tense. In Spanish, the helping verbs cannot be contracted.

The good news for English speakers is that in Spanish, this tense is used in exactly the same way and is formed grammatically in the same manner as in English. English uses the same verb, *to have*, both to mean *to possess* and to function as a helping verb. In Spanish, on the other hand, the verb **haber** is used almost exclusively as a helping verb for all the perfect tenses (those consisting of some form of **haber** plus the past participle of the main verb). The present perfect is only one of seven perfect tenses, all of which will be covered in later chapters.

The name of the tense, *present perfect*, gives us a good sense of its function. From the name *perfect*, we know that some action was performed in the past, since *per* + *factum* means *completely done*. From the word *present*, we learn that somehow, the action performed earlier still exerts some force on the moment of speaking. For this reason, the preceding example, *I have eaten*, is a good one to remember when dealing with the concept of the present perfect. The person is too full to eat again. Hence the prior action, *eating*, is still exerting a force on the speaker at the moment of speaking.

Furthermore, from a morphological point of view, when one refers to a perfect tense in English or Spanish, by definition it can only be a tense that is formed using some form of *have* or **haber**, plus a past participle. The present perfect is formed using the present tense of the helping verb **haber** plus the past participle of any verb one wishes to use in the present perfect tense. Here are the forms of the helping verb **haber** in the present tense:

he	hemos
has	habéis
ha	han

The past (or passive) participle of each verb in Spanish is invariable; that is, it has one form only that is used with the various forms of **haber** to form all the perfect tenses. This should be extremely good news for learners. There is a bit more good news. There are only a dozen important irregular past participles.

Past participles

The regular past participles of infinitive verbs ending in **-ar** are formed by dropping the **-ar** and adding **-ado**. The stress is placed on thet next-to-the-last syllable (no written accent is used). Here are a few examples:

hablar	→	hablado
trabajar	→	trabajado
empezar	→	empezado
excavar	→	excavado

The regular past participles of infinitive verbs ending in **-er** and **-ir** share one ending: the **-er** or **-ir** is dropped and changed to **-ido**. The stress is likewise placed on the next-to-the-last syllable, without a written accent, just as with **-ar** verbs. Examine the following examples:

comer	→	comido
vivir	→	vivido
tener	→	tenido
vender	→	vendido
comprender	→	comprendido

There are, as mentioned earlier, a handful of important verbs whose past participles are irregular. In addition to these important verbs, which are listed on the next page, any verb compounded from a verb on the list will also form its past participle in the same way as the listed verb.

> Keep in mind that verbs compounded from a prefix + the nearly unused verb **solver** form their past participles ending in **-suelto**, such as **absolver → absuelto** and **resolver → resuelto**. One way to remember this is to notice that they rhyme with the past participle of **volver**, which is **vuelto**.

abrir	→	abierto
cubrir	→	cubierto
decir	→	dicho
escribir	→	escrito
freír	→	frito
hacer	→	hecho
morir	→	muerto
poner	→	puesto
romper	→	roto
ver	→	visto
volver	→	vuelto

In addition to the verbs on the list above, the verb **imprimir** (*to print*, as in a printing press or laser printer) has two acceptable past participles: **impreso** and **imprimido**, the latter being more common in Latin America for forming the perfect tenses and the former preferred by the Spanish Royal Academy. However, **impreso** is used everywhere as the base adjective, such as in the expression **una etiqueta impresa** (*a printed label*).

When a reflexive verb is conjugated in any of the perfect tenses in modern Spanish, except in cases of rare rhetorical flourishes, the reflexive object pronoun is always placed before the helping verb. Observe the following examples:

Su perro **se ha muerto**.	*His dog **has died**.*
Las niñas **se han vestido** solas.	*The little girls **have dressed themselves**.*
¿No **te has bañado** ya?	*Haven't you **bathed** yet?*
Nos hemos levantado temprano.	*We **have gotten up** early.*

The name *participle* helps learners understand an important fact about the use of this form, namely that participles *participate* in two grammatical functions. One could say they have a double life. When the past participles are used with **haber** to form the *perfect tenses*, as we have just been discussing, they are invariable in form and participate in the language as part of a *verbal construction*. In that role, they have no gender and their ending in **-o** is not to be considered a gender marker of any kind.

Participle used to form perfect tenses: Invariable participle

He hablado todo el día.	*I **have spoken** all day.*
Han construido la casa.	*They **have built** the house.*
¿**Has hecho** la tarea?	*Have you **done** the homework?*

On the other hand, these participles also participate in the language as *adjectives*, in which case the ending is modified to agree with the noun or nouns they modify in gender and number. This occurs in three ways. First, a participle can function as an adjective, directly following the noun. Secondly, a participle can function as a predicate adjective, following some form of a *be* verb (i.e., **ser** or **estar**). (It often helps to view the *be* verb as an equals sign between the noun-subject and the adjective in the predicate [i.e., the adjective that follows the *be* verb].) Finally, a participle can be the participial component of a passive construction. In distinguishing the passive construction from constructions with *be* verbs and participles used as predicate adjectives, note that true passive constructions can only be formed with **ser** as the *be* verb. The following examples use the past participles in the feminine form, including one in the plural as well, to show more clearly how and when they function as adjectives in the three situations just described.

Past participle as an adjective

Tengo muchas **cartas escritas** por mi abuelo.	*I have many **letters written** by my grandfather.*

Past participle as a predicate adjective

La **tienda está abierta** todos los días.	*The **shop is open** every day.*

Past participle in a passive voice construction

La **casa fue construida** por los carpinteros.	*The **house was built** by the carpenters.*

EJERCICIO
4·1

Indicate whether the past participles in the following sentences are verbal constructions (V), purely adjectival—modifying a noun directly (A), a predicate adjective (PA), or a true passive construction (TP).

1. _____ Hay pocos políticos que siempre han dicho la verdad.

2. _____ La ventana está abierta.

3. _____ Estos productos fueron hechos en México.

4. _____ Puesto el yelmo y probada la espada, Don Quixote salió del corral.

5. _____ Tengo varios libros escritos en el siglo XIX.

6. _____ La madre de ese chico ha desaparecido.

7. _____ Juan ha cerrado la puerta.

8. _____ Hemos hecho todo lo que tuvimos que hacer.

9. _____ Juan y María están casados.

10. _____ La estatua fue puesta en su lugar por los veteranos.

11. _____ Se me ha roto la bicicleta.

12. _____ Los niños fueron llevados a la cama llorando.

13. _____ Juan y María fueron premiados por sus contribuciones a la medicina.

14. _____ Esos muchachos se han puesto las botas para montar a caballo.

15. _____ Los náufragos tenían muchas cosas improvisadas para ayudarles a preparar la cena.

16. _____ ¿Has visto el Mar Rojo alguna vez?

17. _____ El carro está descompuesto ahora.

18. _____ Se han impreso los materiales para la campaña publicitaria.

19. _____ Los primeros rascacielos fueron construidos en Nueva York y Chicago.

20. _____ JFK está muerto.

EJERCICIO
4·2

Write the present perfect of the following verbs, for the subjects indicated.

EXAMPLE   tú/hablar ___*has hablado*___

1. ella/escribir _____

2. yo/ver _____

3. ellos/correr _____

4. usted/ser _____

5. yo/hacer _____

6. ellos/morirse _____

7. ustedes/ir _____

8. tú/comer _____

9. él/dar _____

10. yo/ponerse _____

11. nosotros/abrir _____

12. vosotros/acostarse _____

13. yo/acostarse _____

14. tú/decir _____

15. usted/dedicarse _____

16. él/romper _____

17. yo/volver _____

18. tú/creer _____

19. ellas/resolver _____

20. nosotros/imprimir _____

Translate the following sentences from Spanish to English.

1. Se nos ha roto el arado.

   _____

2. No le ha dicho la verdad a su novio.

   _____

3. Visto el espectáculo, se fueron de la carpa.

   _____

4. Debido a la tormenta, se ha caído un árbol enorme en el parque.

   _____

5. Ella se ha casado con Juan.

   _____

6. Están cansados los niños porque han jugado toda la tarde.

   _____

7. No he visto maravilla, pues; porque no he ido a Sevilla nunca.

   _____

8. Ha habido tantos que han sido encarcelados en los últimos años que hay una
   nueva prisión construida en otro pueblo cercano.

   _____

   _____

9. Tu amigo, ¿ha hecho la tarea?

   _____

10. Tenemos la casa abierta desde las cuatro de la tarde hasta las seis, durante el
    verano.

   _____

11. He puesto un nuevo CD de flamenco en el tocador para escucharlo.

   _____

12. Ellos dicen que el problema ha sido resuelto, pero que la máquina dañada
    todavía está en el sitio de construcción.

   _____

   _____

13. El concierto ha empezado.

   _____

14. Pandora ha abierto la caja.

   _____

15. Esa pareja vecina que peleaba tanto ha roto relaciones.

_____

16. ¿Has visto jamás tal desfachatez?

_____

17. Hemos oído hablar mucho de ese político y no nos cae bien.

_____

18. El boxeador se ha caído por tercera vez.

_____

19. No sé lo que has hecho, pero ha causado muchos problemas.

_____

20. María se ha enamorado locamente de él.

_____

Create complete sentences using the following elements, taking care to form the present perfect of the infinitives given.

1. Yo/ver/partido/en la tele/hoy.

_____

2. Sus jefes/darle/un aumento de sueldo.

_____

3. Ellos/siempre/vivir/en esta ciudad.

_____

4. Tú/hacer/todo/trabajo.

_____

5. Yo/poner/papeles en la mesa.

   _____

6. Mi madre/preparar/cena fantástica.

   _____

7. ¿Adónde/ir/mi perro?

   _____

8. El periódico/ser/impreso.

   _____

9. Nosotros/escribir/carta/abuelos.

   _____

10. Los niños/ponerse/los zapatos, ¡por fin!

    _____

11. Ella/romperse/la pierna. No debe esquiar.

    _____

12. Él/competir/su hermano/desde que estaban en la secundaria.

    _____

13. Ella/vestirse/para ir/baile.

    _____

14. Ellos/imprimir/el periódico.

    _____

15. Las modelos/maquillarse/y están listas para exhibir los nuevos estilos.

    _____

16. El carro/chocarse/árbol.

    _____

17. Su abuelo/morirse.

    _____

18. Su relación/acabarse.

_____

19. Ella/perder/llaves.

_____

20. Susana/decir/mentira.

_____

This is a two-step exercise. First, translate the following sentences from English to Spanish. Second, rewrite the sentences, replacing any and all object nouns with the appropriate object pronouns, taking care not to confuse objects of verbs with objects of prepositions. It is a good idea to use a dictionary to learn the many useful nouns in these examples. For some items, there will be only one sentence.

1. The teacher has brought us the cake.

_____

_____

2. The cat has eaten the bird.

_____

_____

3. We have written the letters to our customers.

_____

_____

4. The managers have given him a promotion and a raise.

_____

_____

5. The driver of the cab has taken me to my favorite hotel.

   _____

   _____

6. The secretaries have put the documents in the file.

   _____

   _____

7. I have listened to the song.

   _____

   _____

8. The judge has died.

   _____

   _____

9. You (**tú**) have told her the truth.

   _____

   _____

10. We have found out (**saber**) what she has done to him.

    _____

    _____

11. Have you (**ustedes**) read the news?

    _____

    _____

12. They have tried (**tratar de**) to buy the stocks.

    _____

    _____

13. What have you (**tú**) told them?

    _____

    _____

14. She has broken the toy.

_____

_____

15. Have they repaired the computer?

_____

_____

16. I have returned to the city.

_____

_____

17. My friends have sent me a gift.

_____

_____

18. They have gone fishing.

_____

_____

19. Susana and Juan have separated.

_____

_____

20. I have seen her in the grocery store.

_____

_____

The pluperfect
What happened before something else

5

The pluperfect is best described and understood as "the past of the past." In both English and Spanish it is the tense used to express the proper sequence of two or more past events regardless of which is actually mentioned first. Without the pluperfect, expressing the sequence of multiple events in the past would require the use of the simple past tense, in the actual sequence of events. It is often more economical to use simple past tenses in the actual order anyway, particularly when dealing with cause and effect, as the following examples show:

El carro **se coleó** y **se chocó** con el ciclista.	*The car **skidded** and **hit** the cyclist.*
Rompió la ola y el surfeador **se cayó**.	*The wave **broke** and the surfer **fell**.*
Juan **estudió** y **aprobó** la clase.	*John **studied** and **passed** the class.*

On the other hand, if two past events are unrelated, using the pluperfect eliminates ambiguity for intelligent speakers of English and Spanish. In other words, the use of the pluperfect allows a speaker to avoid communicating a mistaken impression that one event in the past caused another. The examples below demonstrate how the cause-and-effect relationships expressed in the first two sentences above are undone by the use of the pluperfect; in the sentences below, note also that, instead of **y** (*and*), the temporal adverb **cuando** (*when*) serves to link the two verbs and further reinforces that one event did not cause the other. And note that when the pluperfect and the simple past are used together, their relative positions in the sentence do not affect the meaning:

Cuando el carro **se coleó**, ya **se había chocado** con el ciclista.	*When the car **skidded**, it **had** already **hit** the cyclist.*
Se había caído el surfeador cuando **rompió** la ola.	*The surfer **had fallen** when the wave **broke**.*

The first sentence above shows how important the pluperfect can be. The version of the sentence in which two simple past tenses were used communicates that the car skidded *first* and then, as a result of the skidding, hit the cyclist. By stating the situation as a sequence of two past actions (using the preterite), it implies that the skidding was no fault of the driver's and, thus, that hitting the cyclist was an unavoidable accident. However, in the second version of the sentence, when the pluperfect is used with the verb **chocarse** (*to hit* or *crash into*), it is clear that the driver *was* in control of the vehicle *before* hitting the cyclist. It's easy to see how important the pluperfect could be in a courtroom!

Just as the present perfect indicative is formed by using the present tense of the helping verb **haber** plus the invariable past participles (regular and irregular), the pluperfect indicative is formed by using the imperfect indicative of **haber**, plus the *same* invariable past participles. The *imperfect indicative* of **haber** is regular (as is the case with all but three verbs in the language) and always translates as *had*. Looking at this fact from the perspective of an English speaker who needs to put his or her English thoughts into proper Spanish, when going from English to Spanish, the simple English verb form *had* (the past of *to have*) will be rendered by one of the *six* forms of **haber** in the imperfect indicative. Note that the pattern of the verb **haber** in the imperfect is the same as that for all other verbs in the imperfect, in that the first- and third-person singular forms are identical. In order to avoid confusion, it could be helpful to contrast the imperfect of **haber**, shown below, with the present of **haber**, presented in the previous chapter. Here are the conjugations of the imperfect of **haber**:

había	habíamos
habías	habíais
había	habían

There is more good news for English speakers, which should be clear from the examples above: the usage of the pluperfect is the same in both languages. The pluperfect is always and only about expressing an action or event that happened prior to some other past event, expressed in either the preterite or the imperfect. Just as in English, the order of the clauses is unimportant, since the pluperfect explicitly shows the action that happened first:

Todos los melones **se habían vendido** cuando ellos fueron al mercado.	All the melons **had been sold** when they went to the store.
Intentábamos arrancar el carro, pero **se había descompuesto**.	We were trying to start the car, but it **had broken down**.
Ella quería hablar con él, pero **se había dormido**.	She wanted to talk to him but he **had gone to sleep**.
Abrieron la tumba pero **había sido robada**.	They opened the tomb but it **had been robbed**.
Los niños **se habían acostado** cuando vino Santa Claus.	The children **had gone to bed** when Santa Claus came.

Match the following Spanish pluperfect verb forms with their English pluperfect translations.

1. habían hecho   a. they had written

2. había visto   b. he had told

3. habías comido   c. she had seen

4. había puesto   d. they had eaten lunch

5. habíamos hablado   e. he had done

6. había abierto   f. he had gotten up

7. habían almorzado   g. you had opened

8. se había levantado   h. you had eaten

9. habíais dicho   i. we had spoken

10. habías roto   j. they had made

11. se había acostado   k. you had said

12. había dicho   l. you had gone

13. habían escrito   m. he had placed

14. había hecho   n. you had broken

15. habías ido   o. she had gone to bed

Fill in the blanks with the proper pluperfect forms of the verbs in parentheses.

1. Yo sabía que ella me amaba, aunque no me lo _____

    _____ . (decir)

2. Decidimos ir al cine, aunque mi novia ya _____

    _____ la película. (ver)

3. Juan se olvidó de que ya le _____ _____ la pulsera a su esposa. (dar)

4. Afortunadamente, los García _____ _____

   _____ cuando se encendió el bosque. (mudarse)

5. Los exploradores _____ _____ explorar esa región de la selva por varios años cuando recibieron el permiso para hacerlo. (querer)

6. Mis padres estaban listos para salir y vieron que yo _____

   _____ _____ los zapatos. (ponerse)

7. Cuando llegaron a la playa, vieron que Juanita ya _____

   _____ _____ . (irse)

8. El ladrón quiso evitar el cargo pero no fue posible, porque ya todos lo

   _____ _____ cuando abría la ventana. (mirar)

9. La tragedia de su relación fue que cuando él se dio cuenta de cuánto lo quería

   María, ella, desesperada por su aparente indiferencia, le _____

   _____ una carta en la que expresaba su furia sobre su actitud y

   rompió con él. (enviar)

10. Después de subir la montaña, Juan vio que las cuerdas para descender

    _____ _____ _____ .

    (romperse)

11. Cuando murió Lope de Vega, _____ _____ unas 1.800 obras de teatro. (escribir)

12. Después de que el cura lo _____ _____ , el libertino volvió a pecar. (absolver)

13. Las señoras salieron del almacén y se dieron cuenta de que no _____

    _____ . (pagar)

14. No todos los miembros del club de libros _____

    _____ la novela antes de reunirse para discutirla. (leer)

15. Cuando yo volví a la tienda del joyero, vi que _____

_____ el anillo que me gustaba. (vender)

16. Aunque los diplomáticos _____ _____ en son de paz, trajeron opresión. (venir)

17. Nosotros _____ _____ la cama cuando llegó el taxi. (hacer)

18. Me invitaron a cenar, pero ya _____ _____. (comer)

19. Me volví para sostenerla pero ya _____ _____

_____. (caerse)

20. Los médicos _____ _____ al paciente antes de las tres de la tarde. (examinar)

Translate the following sentences from Spanish to English.

1. Cuando el mono llegó al pie del árbol, el tigre ya había llegado.

_____

2. ¡Los astronautas descubrieron que alguien había llegado al planeta antes que ellos!

_____

3. Se dio prisa para llegar al hospital a tiempo, pero su esposa ya había dado a luz cuando llegó.

_____

_____

4. El capitán de la expedición había muerto antes de llegar a la fuente del río.

_____

5. Cuando los primeros seres humanos aparecieron en África, los dinosaurios ya habían desaparecido.

_____

_____

6. Cuando supieron lo que pasaba con la economía, era tarde; ya habían puesto sus fondos en bonos fijos que no iban a poder vender por cinco años.

_____

_____

7. Cuando salió la novela *Persiles* en 1616, Cervantes había muerto.

_____

8. Fui a la tienda a las ocho, pero no la habían abierto sus dueños.

_____

9. Colón no puede considerarse el descubridor del Nuevo Mundo ya que cuando él llegó, hacía milenios que los amerindios lo habían descubierto.

_____

_____

10. Habíamos resuelto el problema con el auto cuando el mecánico vino.

_____

11. Según algunos médicos, cuando se dice que un anciano se cayó y se rompió la cadera, es porque ya se le había roto la cadera, provocando la caída.

_____

_____

12. Cuando Tomás mandó la carta, su novia ya había ido de vacaciones.

_____

13. Los padres les dijeron a sus hijos que los regalos eran de los Tres Reyes Magos, pero ya los habían visto debajo de la cama.

_____

_____

14. Queríamos saber si ya se había hecho el pastel para la fiesta.

_____

15. Alguien había robado la casa porque vimos que la ventana había sido rota desde afuera y la puerta de enfrente había sido abierta desde adentro, por la cual salió el delincuente, sin duda.

_____

_____

_____

16. Cuando el profesor me mencionó la idea, me di cuenta de que nunca lo había pensado.

_____

17. Su esposa quería hablarle un rato más pero él se había dormido.

_____

18. Llegaron varias personas a la venta pero la cocina ya había cerrado.

_____

19. Los niños querían nadar pero ya se había puesto el sol.

_____

20. Eran las tres de la mañana y no me había dormido cuando terminé este ejercicio.

_____

_____

EJERCICIO

5·4

Translate the following sentences from English to Spanish.

1. Dinner was ready but the children had not washed their hands.

_____

2. We climbed the mountain to see the sunrise but it had risen already.

_____

3. The kittens had been born before the party on Saturday.

_____

4. He had decided to tell her about the trip before Tuesday.

_____

5. When she called him, he had already invited her sister to the dance.

_____

6. They returned home at nine, but the movie had ended already.

_____

7. He wanted to surprise her but she had seen the ring already.

_____

8. The children had opened the window before the storm.

_____

9. She had not told him about her other boyfriend when he saw them in the restaurant.

_____

10. When we hung up the phone, I still had not found the article.

_____

11. The train was arriving and they still had not opened the station.

_____

12. He had not died when the war ended.

_____

13. When his grandparents came to the United States, he had not been born yet.

_____

14. My friend had moved before receiving the letter.

_____

15. The article had been written before last Sunday.

_____

16. She had put on her coat when she noticed it was not cold.

   _____

17. My friend and I had never seen the ocean until we were ten years old.

   _____

18. He had not heard of that musical group until he saw a magazine article about them.

   _____

19. When he returned from the war, he found out that his girlfriend had gotten married.

   _____

20. Had you read the reports before the committee met?

   _____

The conditional

What would be and the future of the past

Technically speaking, the conditional is not a tense. This is because it does not convey any notion of, or reference to, the time of an action. It is a *mood*, along with the infinitive, the two participles, the imperatives and the four subjunctives. It is easy to remember that the conditional is a mood by comparing it to its English counterpart, formed by the auxiliary or *modal* verb (a term that refers to *mood*) *would* plus the verb. In English, the modal does not vary its form; that is, it is the same for all subjects. In Spanish, however, the conditional is fully inflected; that is, it is conjugated, and so it shows particular endings for all six grammatical persons and numbers; for this reason, it is convenient and practical to treat it as a tense.

The conditional is rarely used as a stand-alone form, except in informal speech, where it is often used to answer a question. Used in this way, it does not form grammatically complete sentences in either English or Spanish. There is often an implied *if*-clause, usually stated in a question but omitted in the answer:

Los niños **irían** al parque.	*The children **would go** to the park.*
Su padre **compraría** un carro.	*His father **would buy** a new car.*
Una amiga no te **pondría** en la cárcel.	*A friend **wouldn't put** you in jail.*

It is easy to imagine the questions that the above phrases might answer:

*Where **would** the children **go** . . . if they could?*
*What **would** his father **buy** . . . if he had the money?*
***Would** a friend not **put** you in jail . . . even if she could?*

The first lesson to learn from the above examples is that while the English conditional consists of an invariable verb phrase, the Spanish conditional is a one-word form, fully inflected for all persons and numbers. Next, notice that one consequence of the fact that English employs a two-word construction is that, in questions, the subject is placed in between the modal verb *would* and the verb that completes the conditional. Spanish, with its one-word conditional, is much simpler in this regard. For many English-speaking learners of Spanish, these differences can present conceptual hurdles.

The next thing to notice about the conditional in Spanish, which is illustrated in the preceding examples, is that it is formed by adding one set of personal endings directly to the infinitives of each of the three verb families (-**ar**, -**er**, and -**ir** verbs). Since these endings are identical to the imperfect indicative endings of -**er** and -**ir** verbs, in order to prevent confusion, it is very important to keep in mind that the conditional endings are added to the infinitive:

Conditional endings: Add to the infinitive

+ ía	+ íamos
+ ías	+ íais
+ ía	+ ían

Notice that, as in many other tenses, the first- and third-person singular forms are identical. Observe the following conjugations of **hablar**, **comer**, and **vivir**, the three models for regular -**ar**, -**er**, and -**ir** verbs:

hablaría	hablaríamos	comería	comeríamos	viviría	viviríamos
hablarías	hablaríais	comerías	comeríais	vivirías	viviríais
hablaría	hablarían	comería	comerían	viviría	vivirían

Of course, as learners of Spanish have come to expect, there are irregular verbs. Yet when studying the conditional, there are two bits of good news. First, there are only a handful of irregular verbs. Collectively, these irregularities amount to a new stem. The second bit of good news is that these irregular verbs, shown below with their new stems, are also irregular in exactly the same way in the future tense (which is also formed by adding endings to the infinitive). So, learning the conditional well will pay off twice.

INFINITIVE	STEM FOR CONDITIONAL AND FUTURE
decir	dir-
hacer	har-
poner	pondr-
salir	saldr-
tener	tendr-
valer	valdr-
venir	vendr-
caber	cabr-
haber	habr-
poder	podr-
querer	querr-
saber	sabr-

In order to remember these irregular stems more effectively, notice that they have been divided into three groups according to the way in which they may be recognized. First of all, **decir** and **hacer** are simply wild—you'll just have to memorize them as a pair of oddballs. In the second group, however, in which the final letter of the stem is characteristically either an **l** or an **n**, the pattern is that the theme vowel of the infinitive (an **e** or an **i**) is replaced with a **d**. The third group, finally, may be called verbs with a *collapsed infinitive*. They are also all -**er** verbs.

Now that we have examined the morphology, or formation, of the conditional, we may begin to learn how it is used and when. The conditional is used in three situations. First, the conditional is used to express the consequence of a hypothetical statement; secondly, it is used as the future of the past in indirect discourse; and thirdly, it is used to express probability in the past. Fortunately, the first two ways in which the conditional is used are identical to the way English uses the conditional. The third situation has no clear analogue in English.

When the conditional is used to express a hypothesis or contrary-to-fact situation, it is used correlatively, that is, in tandem with an *if*-clause. The verb form used in the *if*-clause is the imperfect subjunctive. This type of sentence is also encountered in formal logic, where it is known as a *counterfactual proposition*. That might sound like a complicated thing, but we use counterfactuals every day. In fact, counterfactuals are the stuff dreams are made of, as we imagine how the world *would* be *if only*. . . . Examine the following sentences, noting how the conditional expresses the consequence—what *would* happen, if the *if*-clause were to become a reality:

Ella me **amaría** si las circunstancias le **permitieran**.	She **would love** me if her circumstances **allowed** her.
Tú me **visitarías** si no **fuera** por nuestras obligaciones familiares.	You **would visit** me if it **weren't** for our family obligations.
Ellos **participarían** en el proceso político si no **tuvieran** que trabajar todo el tiempo.	They **would participate** in the political process if they **didn't have** to work all the time.

The imperfect subjunctive

In order to do many of the items in the exercises, this particular form of the subjunctive will now be presented, in case learners have never seen it or, if they have, by way of review, so that the usage of the conditional that it is used with may be recognized. Another simple name for the imperfect subjunctive is the simple past subjunctive. It is a *past tense* of the *subjunctive mood*, and since it consists of a one-word form, the qualifying term *simple* is used to distinguish it from *compound* forms—the present perfect subjunctive and the pluperfect subjunctive.

To form the *imperfect subjunctive,* begin with the *third-person plural of the preterite* (the **ellos, ellas, ustedes** form). For *all* verbs, simply remove **-on** and replace it with **-a** and begin conjugating again, using it as a new **yo** form, and adding the personal endings.

You may have learned or seen that there is an alternative form of the imperfect subjunctive that ends in **-se**. It is not used in this book, being somewhat more used in literary settings than in speaking in most regions. In any event, the rules for using this alternative form are the same, stylistic matters aside.

Generally, the irregular verbs in the preterite cause more problems than the irregular verbs in the present, because so many verbs have a new stem in the preterite that can't be derived by any logical rules. However, once the new stems are known, the formation of the imperfect subjunctive is uniformly achieved in the following way (as described above): here we use **tener** as an example. First, the third-person plural of the preterite of **tener** is **tuvieron**; remove the **-on** and add **-a**, and then continue as shown below:

tuvier**a**	tuvié**ramos**
tuvier**as**	tuvier**ais**
tuvier**a**	tuvier**an**

It should come as *truly* good news that this rule works perfectly for all three families of verbs, **-ar, -er,** and **-ir,** both regular and irregular, so that the imperfect subjunctive forms of **hablar, comer,** and **vivir** are all formed like the imperfect subjunctive of **tener**. If the formation of the imperfect subjunctive is difficult for learners, it is almost always because they have not learned the preterite. If this is the case for you, refer to these paragraphs often as you do the exercises.

The second situation in which the conditional is used is when an indirect statement is introduced by a verb in a past tense. Within the indirect statement, the conditional expresses an action that was yet to occur, relative to the past point of reference established by the main verb, which inevitably is a verb about communicating. In this situation, the use of the conditional, in its relation to its main past tense verb, is parallel to the relationship between the future and a main verb in the present.

Observe the following sets of sentences. Note first how the verb in the indirect statement (the **que**-clause) changes tense, depending on the tense that introduces the indirect statement. Since the simple future can also be replaced with the periphrastic future, **ir + a +** infinitive, it is also valuable to notice that the use of the conditional in indirect statements in the past can be replaced with the imperfect of **ir + a +** infinitive, i.e., *was* or *were going to*. This too is an alternative in English, making this a little more good news for English-speaking learners of Spanish.

Indirect statement in the present

Juan me **dice** que nos **llamará** al llegar a casa.

*John **tells** me he **will call** us when he gets home.*

Juan me **dice** que nos **va a llamar** al llegar a casa.

*John **tells** me he **is going to call** us when he gets home.*

Indirect statements in the past

Juan me **dijo** que nos **llamaría** al llegar a casa.

*John **told** me he **would call** us when he got home.*

Juan me **dijo** que nos **iba a llamar** al llegar a casa.

*John **told** me he **was going to call** us when he got home.*

Juan me **decía** que nos **llamaría** al llegar a casa.

*John **was telling** me he **would call** us when he got home.*

Juan me **decía** que nos **iba a llamar** al llegar a casa.

*John **was telling** me he **was going to call** us when he got home.*

The third situation in which the conditional is used also parallels another peculiar function of the future tense in Spanish. Just as the future tense is used to express probability in the present, in the second of the following sentences, the conditional is used as a means to express probability in the past. (Notice also that the conditional is not the only way to show probability in the past, as shown by the final example sentence below. For the purposes of the exercises in this chapter, however, use the conditional when dealing with this situation.)

Probability in the present

Juan **estará** en la biblioteca ahora.

*John **is probably** in the library now.*

Probability in the past

Juan **estaría** en la biblioteca anoche.

*John **was probably** in the library last night.*

Es probable que Juan **estuviera** en la biblioteca anoche.

*It's **probable** that John **was** in the library last night.*

Finally, English-speaking learners of Spanish must be cautious whenever the English auxiliary verb *would* is employed. In English, there are four situations in which the modal verb *would* is used. English-speaking learners of Spanish need to be aware of them so that they can select the proper equivalent in Spanish.

As seen in this chapter, the first situation in which both English and Spanish employ the conditional, and in which the English usage of the modal verb *would* is identical to the Spanish usage of the conditional is when there is an implied *if*-clause, which states a hypothesis. In this situation, the English *would* is rendered as the conditional in Spanish, to express the consequence of that hypothetical action expressed in the imperfect subjunctive.

For the second situation in which English uses *would*, the Spanish equivalent is not the conditional. Fortunately, this is one of the easiest situations to recognize. Learners need only reflect a moment before speaking or writing. If *would* is employed as an equivalent of *used to* + infinitive, it is used to refer to habitual or repeated past action and is rendered in Spanish by the imperfect indicative, *not* the conditional:

Cuando éramos niños, **íbamos** a la playa mucho.

*When we were kids, we **would go** to the beach a lot.*

Thirdly, *would* is also used in English to express the future of the past in an indirect statement. In this situation, the conditional is employed in Spanish as a means to express the future from a point of reference in the past, as seen earlier:

Mi padre me dijo que **vendría** más tarde.

*My father told me that he **would come** later.*

The last use of the English modal *would* is found in its use as a subjunctive, appearing in a subordinated clause introduced by a past tense verb to express, for instance, what someone hoped someone else *would* do or what someone hoped something *would* be like. In this case, Spanish uses the imperfect subjunctive:

Esperaba que Juan **viniera** a la fiesta.

*He was hoping that John **would come** to the party.*

Necesitabas un programa que **funcionara** sin problemas.

*You needed a program that **would work** without problems.*

The use of the conditional to express probability in the past has no English equivalent involving the auxiliary verb *would*, and so this situation rarely causes confusion.

Querer, deber, and poder

Finally, now that we have examined the conditional and the formation of the imperfect subjunctive, it is time to make some important observations about the social usage of three important and common helping verbs. When the verbs **querer, deber,** and **poder** are followed by the infinitive, they are being used as helping verbs. The various degrees of politeness involve the use of the simple present indicative, the conditional, or the imperfect subjunctive, as shown on the next page. The observations we are about to make regarding degrees of politeness and the use of these three tenses are limited to these three verbs only, and then only when they are helping verbs, that is, when they are followed by an infinitive.

Also, it is important to remember that when these three verbs are followed by an infinitive, despite the choice of tense and mood, there is no change in the fundamental meaning of these verbs. The use of these three tenses in this situation does not impact even the time of the action or its likeliness. The choice only indicates a degree of politeness. Grammatically and morphologically, this is a small thing, but socially and culturally, it is a big deal. The following English translations of the Spanish examples are intended to indicate the approximate sense or feel of each degree of politeness:

¿Puedes darme la guía telefónica?	*Can you **give** me the telephone book?*
¿Podrías darme la guía telefónica?	***Could** you **give** me the telephone book?*
¿Pudieras darme la guía telefónica?	***Would** you **be so kind as to give** me the telephone book?*

In all three sentences, the meaning or message is the same. The only difference derived from the choice of present, conditional, or imperfect subjunctive in the auxiliary verb **poder** is that the degree of politeness expressed in these examples *increases* as you go *down* the list.

Knowing how **poder** works should make it relatively easy to intuit what impact the same choices have when used with **querer** and **deber**, even while recognizing that adequate translations into English often are elusive and may seem overly polite, pleading, or even obsequious, which they assuredly are *not* in Spanish, unless of course the tone of voice is. Many dictionaries mistakenly translate **deber** as *must*. Because of its meaning, **deber** tends to be found in statements rather than questions. The degree of politeness softens the severity or adds diplomacy to the moral obligation this verb expresses:

¿Quieres acompañarme al cine?	*Do you **want to go** with me to the movies?*
¿Querrías acompañarme al cine?	***Would** you **like to go** with me to the movies?*
¿Quisieras acompañarme al cine?	***Would** you, **please, like to go** with me to the movies?*
Debes estudiar más si quieres sacar buenas notas.	*You **should study** more if you want to get good grades.*
Deberías estudiar más si quieres sacar buenas notas.	*You **ought to study** more if you want to get good grades.*
Debieras estudiar más si quieres sacar buenas notas.	*You **really ought to study** more if you want to get good grades.*

Be sure to learn these three verbs well in the present, conditional, and imperfect subjunctive. Their potential impact on social and cultural relations cannot be overstated, and no number of cross-cultural communications classes or seminars can make up for not being able to use them correctly.

Match each Spanish conditional verb on the left with the corresponding English phrase on the right.

1. traería

2. amaríamos

3. vendría

4. escribiría

5. empezaría

6. saldría

7. pondría

8. no verían

9. gustaría

10. no sabrían

11. romperían

12. querríamos

13. encontraría

14. harías

15. tendría

16. llamarías

17. comerían

18. amaría

19. iríamos

20. no escucharía

a. she would write

b. they would eat

c. I would put

d. he wouldn't listen

e. we would go

f. they would break

g. I would have

h. you would make

i. she would find

j. I would bring

k. you would call

l. I would begin

m. we would love

n. it would please

o. they wouldn't see

p. he would leave

q. she would love

r. we would want

s. she would come

t. they wouldn't know

Fill in the blanks with the proper conditional forms of the verbs in parentheses.

1. Si ella me dijera una mentira, yo _____ en seguida que me miente. (saber)

2. Ayer tú me dijiste que _____ a clase hoy. (asistir)

3. Si Tomás lo viera, lo _____. (creer)

4. No lo sé, parece que ayer Teresa _____ el almuerzo, pero no la vi. (traer)

5. Me _____ conocer a sus amigas; se ven divertidas en la foto. (gustar)

6. Si nos metiéramos de lleno en la materia, _____ mucha riqueza. (encontrar)

7. Uds. me informaron que _____ cumplir con los requisitos del contrato. (poder)

8. Si nosotros no estuviéramos enfermos, _____. (trabajar)

9. A lo mejor mis amigos _____ tiempo para ver la película anoche. (tener)

10. Me pregunto cuántos hombres _____ en la calle esa noche. Era muy tarde y estaba muy oscura. (haber)

11. Si ella estuviera aquí conmigo, yo le _____ cómo me siento. (decir)

12. Ella _____ el grito al cielo si supiera lo que esa mujer me dijo. (poner)

13. Ellos _____ la casa si los precios no fueran tan bajos ahora. (vender)

14. Si el perro pudiera ver al gato, _____ de casa como un relámpago. (salir)

15. ¿Qué _____ tú si no tuvieras que trabajar para vivir? (hacer)

16. _____ médico si su familia diopusiera de fondos para pagar su educación. (ser)

17. Mi padre me dijo que nosotros _____ a la playa si no hiciera mal tiempo. (ir)

18. Si ellos pudieran y se atrevieran, _____ a un acuerdo. (llegar)

19. ¿Por un beso? No sé qué te _____ por un beso. (dar)

20. Yo la _____, si fuera factible. Hay amores imposibles, pero amores son. (querer)

EJERCICIO
6·3

Translate the following sentences from Spanish to English.

1. Los niños pondrían la mesa si su mamá se lo pidiera.

   _____

2. Si no fuera por sus padres, no estaría usted aquí.

   _____

3. El profesor le dijo que ella aprendería mucho en su clase.

   _____

4. Si Ud. quisiera, podría acompañarme al cine, ¡para ver a ese actor a quien dices que me parezco!

   _____

   _____

5. Ese muchacho me dijo que vendría a buscarme a eso de las seis, pero no ha llegado.

   _____

   _____

6. ¿Dónde estaría mi mamá cuando su primo la llamó?

   _____

7. ¿Qué me diría mi esposa si la llamara "mi cielo"?

   _____

8. María escribiría poesía anoche porque está enamorada de él.

   _____

9. Yo bailaría más si no me doliera la rodilla.

   _____

10. Si las suegras se murieran todas, los maridos valdrían más.

    _____

11. Nos gustaría enseñar una clase juntos si pudiéramos hallar un tema interesante.

    _____

12. Ella le dijo a su hijito que lo bañaría pronto.

    _____

13. ¿Te interesaría viajar a París si la línea aérea te diera un boleto gratis?

    _____

14. Yo les prometí a los alumnos que tocaría más música en la clase.

    _____

15. Si yo tocara música cubana, ¿bailarían los alumnos?

    _____

16. ¿Podrías ayudarme a seleccionar las canciones para la clase?

    _____

17. Los alumnos deberían asistir a clase todos los días.

    _____

Translate the following sentences from English to Spanish.

1. She would go to the party if she had time.

   _____

2. They said they would bring the food.

   _____

3. He told me that she would find the manager's phone number.

   _____

4. They were probably in the bookstore when I called.

   _____

5. What would she say to me if she could see me now?

   _____

6. How would you say "It's a beautiful day" in Spanish?

   _____

7. If John were taller, we would ask him to play on our team.

   _____

8. When her boyfriend came home, she was probably studying.

   _____

9. He was probably happy to see her last night.

   _____

10. What would you do if you won the lottery?

    _____

11. My friend said he would read more if he had time.

    _____

12. If their age difference were not an issue, their situation would be different.

    _____

13. I was probably cooking when you called me.

_____

14. Even if the price of homes were to increase a lot, I would not sell mine.

_____

15. The car was probably moving too fast.

_____

16. If I had a horse, I would name him Sirocco.

_____

17. The doctor told me that he would not operate on my knee.

_____

18. The children were probably playing when it began to rain.

_____

19. If I were French, I would think differently about life.

_____

20. I would eat more fish if it did not cost so much.

_____

The conditional perfect

What would have been

7

The conditional perfect performs the same functions as the conditional, except that, like all the perfect tenses, it shifts to the past. If you keep in mind the differences in temporal perspective between the present and the present perfect, you will be able to apply this shift to the other tenses in relation to their respective perfect ones. Thus, just as the conditional speaks of what *would be*, the conditional perfect speaks of what *would have been*. In the same way that the simple conditional often has an implicit *if*-clause in the imperfect subjunctive, the conditional perfect often has an implied *if*-clause in the pluperfect subjunctive.

Taking the same sentences we used to begin our study of the simple conditional in the last chapter, let's see how the sentences change when we shift temporal gears and use the conditional perfect instead. One of the most important things to notice is that the conditional endings are shifted to the helping verb **haber**, and that the main verbs, previously conjugated in the conditional, now assume their past participial forms, as happens uniformly throughout the entire perfect system:

Los niños **habrían ido** al parque.	*The children **would have gone** to the park.*
Su padre **habría comprado** un carro nuevo.	*His father **would have bought** a new car.*
Una amiga no te **habría metido** en la cárcel.	*A friend **would** not **have put** you in jail.*

Let's focus on these specific changes by contrasting the simple conditional forms with those of the conditional perfect:

SIMPLE CONDITIONAL	CONDITIONAL PERFECT
irían	habrían ido
compraría	habría comprado
metería	habría metido

The questions which these phrases answer would of course also have been framed differently, reflecting the shift to the conditional perfect. Observe how the second set of questions on the next page are framed to elicit a conditional perfect response. The questions we saw in the previous chapter were framed in expectation of a simple conditional response:

> *Where **would** the children **go** . . . if they could?*
> *What **would** his father **buy** . . . if he had the money?*
> *What **would** a friend not **do** . . . if she were a friend?*

When framed in expectation of a conditional perfect answer, however, these questions now look like this:

> *Where **would** the children **have gone** . . . if they **could have gone** anywhere?*
> *What **would** his father **have bought** . . . if he **had had** the money?*
> *What **would** a friend not **have done** . . . if she **had been** a friend?*

Now, let's examine the three ways in which we have seen that the conditional is used, but now using the conditional perfect. The hypothetical or counterfactual statements are quite simple. In the contrastive pairs of sentences below, pay close attention to the way that the simple tenses in both clauses are shifted to compound, or perfect tenses, involving the use of **haber** and the past participles. Noticing that the same shift occurs in English should give you confidence in using these tenses:

¿Adónde **irían** los niños si **pudieran** ir a cualquier parte?	*Where **would** the children **go** if they **could** go anywhere?*
¿Adónde **habrían ido** los niños si **hubieran podido** ir a cualquier parte?	*Where **would** the children **have gone** if they **could have** gone anywhere?*
¿Qué **compraría** su padre si **tuviera** el dinero?	*What **would** his father **buy** if he **had** the money?*
¿Qué **habría comprado** su padre si **hubiera tenido** el dinero?	*What **would** his father **have bought** if he **had had** the money?*
Una amiga no te **metería** en la cárcel si **supiera** tus secretos.	*A friend **would** not **put** you in jail if she **knew** your secrets.*
Una amiga no te **habría metido** en la cárcel si **hubiera sabido** tus secretos.	*A friend **would** not **have put** you in jail if she **had known** your secrets.*

Since counterfactuals express circumstances that are *not* the case, the simple tense versions above speak of what is *not* the case *at the moment of speaking*. That is, their time frame is a sort of hypothetical out-of-time, a stepping outside of current realities. The compound versions express that events did not go as expected. They could be seen as existing in a time frame that takes an attitude of "if only such and such had or had not happened."

The second situation that we observed while examining the conditional in Chapter 6 was the use of the conditional in indirect statements introduced by past-tense verbs of *communication*. Compare the use of the simple tenses with what happens to meaning, or perspective, when the conditional perfect is used instead. We now have a past situation similar to that of the use of the simple conditional, but this time it is embedded in the indirect statement: there is an implied *if*-clause:

Juan me **dijo** que nos **llamaría** al llegar a casa.	John **told** me he **would call** us when he got home.
Juan me **dijo** que nos **habría llamado** al llegar a casa...	John **told** me he **would have called** us when he got home . . .

The unsupplied *if*-clause, if expressed, would necessarily be in the pluperfect (or compound past) subjunctive: **...si no *hubiera perdido* su teléfono celular**.

Learners should be aware that in Latin America it is very common for the **-ara** forms of the imperfect subjunctive to be used as an equivalent of the conditional. Thus, the conditional clauses of the above sentences would look as follows, with no change in the use of the imperfect subjunctive in the *if*-clause:

Juan me **dijo** que nos **llamara** al llegar a casa.	John **told** me he **would call** us when he got home.
Juan me **dijo** que nos **hubiera llamado** al llegar a casa si no hubiera perdido su teléfono celular.	John **told** me he **would have called** us when he got home if he had not lost his cellphone.

The third situation we saw when examining the conditional was the use of the conditional for expressing probability in the past. When the conditional perfect is used, the probability of the event expressed is one that might have happened prior to something else, expressed or implied. What is to be observed is that when the moment in question is more remote relative to the moment of speaking, the compound conditional is used. As observed previously, this is not the only way of expressing probability in the past, as the following pairs of sentences show:

Juan **estaría** en la biblioteca anoche.	John **was probably** in the library last night.
Es probable que Juan **estuviera** en la biblioteca anoche.	**It's probable** that John **was** in the library last night.
Juan **habría estado** en la biblioteca aquella noche.	John **had probably been** in the library that night.
Era probable que Juan **hubiera estado** en la biblioteca aquella noche.	**It was probable** that John **had been** in the library that night.

Because of the close and logical relationship between the simple conditional and the perfect conditional, most of the items in the following set of exercises will be adaptations of the exercises of the previous chapter. That is, the sentences will merely shift the time of the action into the past by using the conditional perfect.

Match each Spanish conditional verb on the left with the corresponding English phrase on the right.

1. habrían traído   a. they would have gone out

2. habríamos amado   b. you would not have seen

3. habríamos venido   c. we would have broken

4. habría escrito   d. you would have wanted

5. habría empezado   e. I would have found

6. habrían salido   f. we would not have listened

7. habríamos puesto   g. we would have had

8. no habrían visto   h. she would have loved

9. habría gustado   i. he would have written

10. no habrías sabido   j. she would have begun

11. habríamos roto   k. we would have loved

12. habrías querido   l. you would have eaten

13. habría encontrado   m. you would have made

14. habrías hecho   n. they would have gone

15. habríamos tenido   o. they would have brought

16. habrían llamado   p. they would have called

17. habría comido   q. we would have placed

18. habría amado   r. it would have pleased

19. habrían ido   s. you would not have found out

20. no habríamos escuchado   t. we would have come

Fill in the blanks with the proper conditional or conditional perfect forms of the verbs in parentheses.

1. Si ella me hubiera dicho una mentira, yo _____ en seguida que me mentía. (saber)

2. Tú me habías dicho que _____ a clase la semana pasada si no hubiera sido por la gripe. (asistir)

3. Si Tomás lo hubiera visto, lo _____ . (creer)

4. No lo sabía, pero parecía que Teresa _____ el almuerzo pronto. (traer)

5. Me _____ conocer a sus amigas; se veían divertidas en la foto. (gustar)

6. Si nos hubiéramos metido de lleno en la materia, _____ mucha riqueza. (encontrar)

7. Uds. me informaron que _____ cumplir con los requisitos del contrato antes de la fecha límite. (poder)

8. Si nosotros no hubiéramos estado enfermos ese día, _____ . (trabajar)

9. A lo mejor mis amigos _____ tiempo para ver la película antes de volver al aeropuerto. (tener)

10. Me pregunté cuántos hombres _____ la escena antes de llegar la policía. (abandonar)

11. Si ella hubiera estado aquí conmigo, yo le _____ cómo me sentía. (decir)

12. Ella _____ el grito en el cielo si hubiera sabido lo que esa mujer me había dicho. (poner)

13. Ellos _____ la casa antes del verano si los precios no hubieran sido tan bajos. (vender)

14. Si el perro hubiera podido ver al gato, _____ de casa como un relámpago. (salir)

15. ¿Qué _____ tú ese año si no hubieras tenido que trabajar tanto? (hacer)

The conditional perfect   **77**

16. _____ médico si su familia hubiera dispuesto de fondos para pagar su educación. (ser)

17. Mi padre me dijo que nosotros _____ a la playa si no hubiera hecho mal tiempo ese día. (ir)

18. Si ellos hubieran podido, _____ a un acuerdo. (llegar)

19. ¿Por un beso? No sé qué te _____ por un beso esa noche. (dar)

20. Yo la _____, si hubiera sido factible. Aprendí que hay amores imposibles, pero amores son y son eternos. (querer)

EJERCICIO

7·3

Translate the following sentences from Spanish to English.

1. Los niños habrían puesto la mesa si su mamá se lo hubiera pedido.

   _____

2. Si no hubiera sido por sus padres, no habrías nacido, claro.

   _____

3. El profesor le dijo que ella habría aprendido mucho en su clase si se hubiera dedicado a los estudios.

   _____

4. Si Ud. hubiera querido, habría podido acompañarme al cine esa noche, ¡para ver a ese actor a quien dices que me parezco!

   _____

5. Ese muchacho me confesó que habría venido a buscarme a eso de las seis, pero que no pudo porque su coche se descompuso.

   _____

6. Nos preguntábamos dónde habría estado mi mamá cuando por fin llegó a casa.

   _____

7. ¿Qué me habría dicho mi esposa si la hubiera llamado "mi cielo" cuando estaba enojada?

   _____

8. María habría escrito poesía ese verano porque estaba enamorada de él.

   _____

9. Yo habría bailado más si no me hubiera dolido tanto la rodilla.

   _____

10. Si las suegras se hubieran muerto todas, los maridos habrían valido más.

    _____

11. Nos habría gustado enseñar una clase juntos ese año si hubiéramos podido hallar un tema interesante.

    _____

12. Ella le dijo a su hijito que lo habría bañado pero no había suficiente agua caliente.

    _____

13. ¿Te habría interesado viajar a París el otoño pasado si la línea aérea te hubiera dado un boleto gratis?

    _____

14. Yo les aseguré a los alumnos que habría tocado más música en la clase si no hubiera sido por la clase de enfrente.

    _____

15. Si yo hubiera tocado música cubana, ¿habrían bailado los alumnos?

    _____

16. ¿Habrías podido ayudarme a seleccionar las canciones para la clase si hubiéramos podido tocarlas?

    _____

17. Los alumnos habrían asistido a clase todos los días si no hubiera sido por las muchas distracciones de la ciudad.

    _____

Translate the following sentences from English to Spanish.

1. She would have gone to the party if she had had time.

   _____

2. They said they would have brought the food, but that they did not have enough money.

   _____

3. He told me that she would have found the manager's phone number if she had not lost her purse.

   _____

4. They had probably been in the bookstore, because when I called, they mentioned they had found an interesting novel.

   _____

5. What would she have said if she had been able to see me then?

   _____

6. How would you have said "It's a beautiful day" in Spanish?

   _____

7. If John had been taller, we would have asked him to play on our team.

   _____

8. She had probably been studying when her boyfriend came home, because all her books were on the table.

   _____

9. He had probably been waiting to see her all night.

   _____

10. What would you have done if you had won the lottery?

    _____

11. My friend said he would have read more if he had had the time when he was young.

   _____

12. If the difference in their ages had not been an issue, their situation would have been different.

   _____

13. When you called him, he had probably been cooking because he talked about dinner a lot.

   _____

14. Even if the price of homes had increased a lot, I would not have sold mine.

   _____

15. The car had probably been moving too fast.

   _____

16. If I had had a horse, I would have named him Sirocco.

   _____

17. The doctor told me that he would not have operated on my knee if it had not hurt so much.

   _____

18. The children had probably been playing all morning when it began to rain.

   _____

19. If I had been French, I would have thought differently about life.

   _____

20. I would have eaten more fish if I had known it was so healthful.

   _____

The sequence of tenses

Observations on the indicative and the subjunctive

Now that you have gone through all the past tenses, as well as the simple conditional and the conditional perfect, and contrasted their uses in terms of point of view, we need to take a close look at what is known as sequence of tenses. Understanding which tenses can or must be used in subordinated clauses, introduced by main clauses in which the various indicative tenses are used, will enable you to choose and use the proper indicative or subjunctive form for each context.

In order to master Spanish, you need to comprehend the *temporal logic* of all tenses, including the four tenses of the subjunctive mood. When dealing with a choice between the indicative and the subjunctive, you'll discover that whether to use the subjunctive at all is the first choice you have to make, and is a separate issue from the question of tense; once the choice is made to use the subjunctive, then the choice of which subjunctive to use has to do with temporal logic. The same temporal logic applies as well to the choice of indicative tense, when the indicative is required. Once this logic is clear, you will have the confidence to tackle the exercises in which any tense and mood could be needed.

Whether or not this is your first exposure to the subject, it is good to clarify what is meant by sequence of tenses. We'll begin with an illustration of the rules for sequence of tenses by comparing four sentences. In order to foreground the issue of sequence of tenses, we will be examining sentences in which the subjunctive *and* indicative moods will be contrasted.

In order to model the temporal logic of the tenses and moods in Spanish, we will be using verbs of emotion and verbs that merely report information, in various tenses, in a series of main, or independent, clauses to introduce subordinate clauses. Verbs of these types provide the necessary flexibility with respect to temporal contexts. As you will see, the tense of the main clause establishes the time frame for the rest of the sentence and thus, the tense of any verb that follows will have been determined by that main verb. Whether the subjunctive mood is needed or not will depend on what type of subordinated clause the main verb introduces. To keep things simple, we will only use verbs of emotion in the examples involving the subjunctive, in order to illustrate how one goes about deciding which of the four tenses of the subjunctive mood will be required in the respective subordinated clauses. When verbs of reporting or informing are used, some indicative tense will be needed. By contrasting such sentences, we will be able to reveal the principle of sequence of tenses, and hopefully you will be able to internalize the logic of this principle.

It is highly advisable to *memorize the examples that follow, along with their translations*, so you have a number of different models on the tip of your tongue. *Use* these examples as models for sentences of your own. They *need* to be in your head so you can learn to express your own thoughts; after all, we only truly know what we can remember and use. The good news is that these are the only patterns there are for the management of the sequence of tenses. In a nutshell, don't overanalyze!

In both of the following examples, the party could either be being planned or already be in progress. Either way, the main clause of the first example contains a verb of emotion in the present indicative, therefore requiring whatever verb is in the subordinated clause to be in the present tense, but in the subjunctive mood. The verb in the main clause of the second example is not a verb that will cause the subjunctive to be necessary. However, what matters for the purpose of understanding the sequence of tenses here is the fact that the time frame is the present and that, therefore, the verbs of the subordinated clauses must be in the present, regardless of mood:

Me alegro de que Juan **venga** a la fiesta.	*I am glad that John **is coming** to the party.*
Sé que Juan **viene** a la fiesta.	*I know that John **is coming** to the party.*

If the party is definitely in progress, then the present perfect, in either the indicative or subjunctive mood, is used to express an action that has taken place and whose influence is still in effect. Thus, in the following examples, the party is actually going on; the speaker either has or has not seen John:

Me alegro de que Juan **haya venido** a la fiesta.	*I am glad that John **has come** to the party.*
Veo que Juan **ha venido** a la fiesta.	*I see that John **has come** to the party.*

In the first of the following four examples, the speaker uses the imperfect subjunctive to express a strong doubt about John's attendance at the party. There are two possible scenarios. First, if the party is in progress, the speaker views John's arrival as so highly unlikely, or contrary to the current reality, that he or she uses the imperfect subjunctive. In this scenario, the use of the imperfect subjunctive is temporally equal to the present perfect subjunctive in the first example above and, in fact, the speaker could have used that form to express the same doubt. The second scenario is that the party is *over* and the speaker expresses his or her current doubts about John's attendance. The second and third examples below express certainties; therefore, no subjunctives are used. The fourth example is a reminder about the use of the conditional as the future of the past in an indirect statement:

Dudo que Juan **viniera** a la fiesta.	*I doubt that John **has come** to the party.* *I doubt that John **came** to the party.*
Sé que Juan **vino** a la fiesta.	*I know that John **came** to the party.*
Sé que Juan **venía** a la fiesta.	*I know that John **was coming** to the party.*
Juan me dijo que **vendría** a la fiesta.	*John said he **would come** to the party.*

More commonly, the imperfect subjunctive is used in subordinated clauses introduced by a verb in a past tense in the main or independent clause (either preterite or imperfect indicative), just as the present subjunctive is used in clauses subordinated to a main clause whose verb is in the present indicative. Compare the following two examples:

Dudo que Juan **venga**...	*I doubt that John **will come** . . .*
Dudaba que Juan **viniera**...	*I doubt that John **would come/was coming** . . .*

In both cases, John's arrival is in the future—*relative to the time of the utterance.*

The pluperfect subjunctive is used for an action that is viewed as prior to some other action in the past. Thus, in the following examples, the party is not only over, but in the first case, in which the speaker's *past* doubt is expressed, John's arrival is viewed as something that (logically) would have had to have occurred before the party ended. In other words, and quite simply—John never showed up. Note that the speaker reports his or her doubt as a past state of mind, clearly establishing the past time frame:

Dudaba que Juan **hubiera venido** a la fiesta.	*I doubted that John **had come** to the party.*
Vi que Juan **había venido** a la fiesta.	*I saw that John **had come** to the party.*

The temporal logic needed to manage the sequence of tenses can be seen in other easily recognized independent clauses where verbs of disbelief or doubt are used in different tenses, in the independent clause, to introduce the subordinate clause. The following comparative summary shows the usage of the four subjunctive tenses and how they are related temporally to the seven indicative tenses and the two conditional ones (simple and compound). You might want to review these tenses as you examine these examples.

The sentences on the left serve as reminders that not all types of verbs in an independent clause will necessitate the use of the subjunctive in the subordinate clause. Remember, it is the verb in the main clause that sets the time frame, regardless of whether the indicative or subjunctive mood must be used.

Indicative	Subjunctive
Creo que ella **viene**.	No creo que ella **venga**.
*I believe she **is coming**.*	*I don't believe she **is coming** (or **will come**).*
Creo que ella **vendrá**.	No creo que ella **venga**.
*I believe she **will come**.*	*I don't believe she **is coming** (or **will come**).*

In the previous two examples, the present subjunctive has both present *and* future force.

Indicative	Subjunctive
Creo que ella **ha venido**.	No creo que ella **haya venido**.
*I believe she **has come**.*	*I don't believe she **has come**.*

As a comparison of the Spanish and English in the above examples shows, it is best to view the subjunctive as a form that has no meaning of its own—it's just a verb form that has to be used in certain situations, but one that has four tenses that must be used according to the temporal logic of the verb system. Also note that the present perfect indicative (*has come* = **ha venido**) has its corresponding subjunctive form (*has come* = **haya venido**) to be used when the subjunctive is necessary.

Indicative	Subjunctive
Creo que ella **habrá venido**.	No creo que ella **haya venido**.
*I believe she **has come**.*	*I don't believe she **has come**.*

Note that in the example on the left, above, the *future perfect* in Spanish indicates probability in the present—one of the peculiar uses of the future tenses in Spanish, as we have seen when examining the conditional and how it is used in the same way as the future, but for indicating probability in the past. A somewhat longer English translation would insert the word *probably* or some other word to express wonder or supposition.

Indicative	Subjunctive
Creo que ella **vino**.	No creo que ella **viniera**.
*I believe she **came**.*	*I don't believe she **came** (or **has come**).*

The example on the right, above (the last in which the present tense is used in the independent clause), shows how a belief or disbelief can be expressed in the present about a past event. The Spanish use of the imperfect subjunctive (**viniera**) in this example contrasts very slightly with the previous example, in which the present perfect subjunctive (**haya venido**) was used. The choice depends on the remoteness of the event. The same reasoning is used in English when deciding between simple past (*came*) and present perfect (*has* come). The only additional factor in Spanish is that each of these English words has both indicative and subjunctive equivalents in Spanish, depending on the clauses in which they appear.

Indicative	Subjunctive
Creí que ella **venía**.	No creí que ella **viniera**.
*I believed she **was coming**.*	*I didn't believe she **would come**.*

In the above examples, the sentence on the left is a good example of the contrast between *preterite* (indicative) and *imperfect* (indicative). The preterite is used to indicate a moment in the past when the speaker's belief about something occurred. The action expressed by the *imperfect indicative* could express her arrival as being either in progress, with respect to the moment of speaking, or else still in the future, as is also the case in the English translation of this example. The example on the right only changes that belief to a disbelief.

What is especially noteworthy is not that the imperfect subjunctive must be used, but that when the imperfect subjunctive is introduced by a past-tense verb in the independent clause, the action expressed by the imperfect subjunctive can only refer to an action unfolding or yet to occur—it becomes another future-of-the-past tense, just like the conditional in indirect statements introduced by a verb in a past tense. However, when introduced by a *present*-tense verb, as seen on page 85, the imperfect subjunctive can only refer to an action in the *past*. Whether or not the action occurred or not is irrelevant from a grammatical point of view.

Indicative	Subjunctive
Creí que ella **vendría**.	No creí que ella **viniera**.
*I believed she **would come**.*	*I didn't believe she **would come**.*

The only difference between the left-hand example above and the left-hand example in the previous set is the use of the conditional (**vendría**) instead of the *imperfect indicative* (**venía**). Just as the *future* tense was used earlier to indicate probability in the present, one peculiar use of the conditional in Spanish is to indicate probability in the past. When changing an expression of belief in the past to an expression of disbelief in the past, the grammatical consequence for the subordinate clause remains the same—the imperfect subjunctive must be used.

Indicative	Subjunctive
Creía que ella **vino**.	No creía que ella **viniera**.
*I believed she **came**.*	*I didn't believe she **would come**.*

In the examples above, the *imperfect indicative* was used instead of the *preterite* for the verb in the independent clause. This choice has *no* impact on the subjunctive used in the example on the right, where the belief shifts to disbelief. The lesson here is that when the verb in the independent clause is in any past tense, the present and present perfect subjunctives simply are not admissible choices in Spanish because they purport to occur in a time frame that is impossible from the temporal perspective of the main verb. Consider how illogical it is to *command* someone to have *already* done something, and the problems involved when dealing with sequence of tenses will be obvious immediately.

However, as previous examples have shown, when *present*-tense verbs are used in the independent clause, the verb in the subordinate or dependent clause can be in any tense, depending on logic. As was just observed, while it would be illogical to demand that something have happened already, it is perfectly possible to wish, in the here-and-now, for something to *happen* or to *have happened*, or to wish it *had happened* (*prior* to something else, please note!), depending on context.

Indicative	Subjunctive
Creía que ella **había venido**.	No creía que ella **hubiera venido**.
*I believed she **had come**.*	*I didn't believe she **had come**.*
Creía que ella **habría venido**.	No creía que ella **hubiera venido**.
*I believed she **had come**.*	*I didn't believe she **had come**.*

The two pairs of examples above are like two previous pairs of examples (**Creo que ella vino/No creo que ella viniera** and **Creí que ella vendría/No creí que ella viniera**). The difference is that in these last two pairs of examples, displayed above, the action is shifted further into the past by the use of **haber** + past participle. Also, just as the present perfect indicative (**ha venido**) has a corresponding subjunctive form, namely the present perfect subjunctive (**haya venido**), the pluperfect indicative (**había venido**) also has its own corresponding subjunctive form, namely the pluperfect subjunctive (**hubiera venido**).

Now that we have examined all the past tenses and moods, the following exercises will test your knowledge of all tenses and moods of the Spanish verb system.

EJERCICIO
8·1

Fill in the blanks with the proper tenses and moods of the verbs in parentheses.

1. Vi que los perros no _____ concentrarse para cazar ya que

   _____ mucha hambre. (poder/tener)

2. Ellos _____ que tú y Jaime _____ a ver la
   película con ellos ayer. (esperar/ir)

3. Mi amigo me _____ que era importante que yo

   _____ ese programa pronto. (decir/ver)

4. Anoche, yo le _____ que _____ urgente que

   ella _____ el artículo antes de ir a clase. (decir/ser/leer)

5. ¿_____ tú que ellos _____ la cuenta en
   efectivo ahora? (querer/pagar)

6. Ella _____ la lección para que te la _____
   enseñar mañana. (estudiar/poder)

7. Cuando Juan me _____ ayer que ellos _____

   _____ un libro traducido, yo _____ que ellos

   _____ _____ el libro antes de 2000.

   (mencionar/publicar/dudar/traducir)

8. _____ obvio que tú _____ _____
   tantos poemas desde 2006. (ser/escribir)

9. Él no _____ una novia que le _____ mentiras.
   (querer/decir)

10. El día de su santo, el fin de semana pasado, mi amiga nos _____

    que le _____ "Las mañanitas". (pedir/cantar)

11. Yo _____ que _____ fantástico que tú

    _____ para mi padre. (creer/ser/trabajar)

12. El año pasado, no les _____ nada que tú y yo

    _____ _____ a nuestros trabajos antes de la

    Navidad. (gustar/renunciar)

Multiple choice. Select the subordinate clause that would correctly complete each of the following main clauses, according to the logic of the sequence of tenses.

1. El ingeniero quería que
   a. su jefe les ayudara a encontrar los materiales necesarios.
   b. su compañero le dé mejores consejos.
   c. sus padres hayan venido a visitarle más.
   d. tenga más tiempo libre.

2. Juana vio que su novio
   a. le va a comprar flores el día de su santo.
   b. la llama todos los días.
   c. sepa bailar bien.
   d. le había comprado un regalo romántico.

3. Mi familia y yo buscábamos una playa en que
   a. pudiéramos alquilar tablas de surf.
   b. hace sol.
   c. no había mucha gente.
   d. no llovía nunca.

4. Tus profesores te han recomendado que tú
   a. te hubieras quedado en casa ese fin de semana.
   b. no comieras tanto.
   c. duermas más de noche.
   d. compraras un nuevo abrigo.

5. No había ningún político que
   a. pague más impuestos que yo.
   b. se atreviera a decir que los pobres deberían trabajar sin descanso.
   c. pensaba que la clase media tenga que pagar más impuestos.
   d. decía que los ricos sean superiores a los demás ciudadanos.

6. Mis amigos llamaron a mi padre antes de que mi madre
   a. pueda preparar la cena.
   b. haya tenido tiempo para descansar.
   c. pudiera ver el noticiero.
   d. pueda regresar del trabajo.

7. Yo iba a ir al cine tan pronto como
   a. tú vengas a buscarme en el coche.
   b. tú pudieras venir a buscarme en el coche.
   c. tú y tus amigos hayan tenido tiempo para ver una película.
   d. yo pueda ponerme los zapatos.

8. Sus padres le dijeron a Jaime que
   a. le regalarían un coche con tal de que sacara mejores notas en la universidad.
   b. encuentre mejor trabajo.
   c. no se graduaba de la universidad.
   d. no se case con Juana.

9. Yo podré irme a Europa a menos que
   a. no tuviera suficientes fondos disponibles.
   b. hiciera mal tiempo en París.
   c. hace mal tiempo en París.
   d. tenga que trabajar durante esa semana.

10. Uds. habrían puesto la mesa si
    a. tengan tiempo antes de que empiece el programa en la tele.
    b. su mamá se lo hubiera pedido.
    c. han visto que no hay cubiertos limpios.
    d. hayan visto los cubiertos limpios.

EJERCICIO
8·3

Fill in the blanks with the proper forms of the verbs in parentheses. If a verb in parentheses is reflexive, don't forget to use the correct pronoun.

1. Mientras _____ ahora, yo _____ a dormir en el sofá. (nevar/ir)

2. Después de _____, mis amigos _____ correr cinco millas. (nadar/decidir)

3. Generalmente cuando Juan _____ cartas, su esposa

   _____ la tele. (escribir/mirar)

4. ¿Qué _____ él que quería que tú _____ después de ver la película? (decir/hacer)

5. Hasta que se murió de vieja, ella _____ en él todas las noches

   aunque _____ que no lo _____ hasta

   abrazarlo en el más allá. (pensar/saber/ver)

6. ¿Dónde _____ los testigos cuando tú _____

   del accidente? (estar/saber)

7. Para concluir, _____ obvio ahora que John Lennon

   _____ un músico talentoso. (ser/ser)

8. Por mucho que los exploradores _____ hacerlo, nunca

   _____ escalar esa montaña el año pasado. (querer/poder)

9. Aunque su madre le _____ _____ que no lo

   _____, mientras Caperucita Roja _____ por el

   bosque, _____ flores. (decir/hacer/ir/recoger)

10. Yo lo _____ _____ ayer, si _____

    _____ suficientes ganas de hacerlo. (hacer/tener)

11. Cuando nosotros lo _____ ayer, me iba preguntando dónde

    _____, pero no lo _____ por mucho que lo

    _____. (buscar/estar/encontrar/buscar)

12. Fidel Castro siempre _____ por siete horas cuando

    _____ discursos en público. (hablar/dar)

13. Mientras _____ el sol ese día, nosotros _____

    cuenta de que _____ hambre, así que _____

    al Plato de Oro. (ponerse/darse/tener/ir)

14. Tras varios años de noviazgo, Amaranta _____ que no

    _____ con Crespi. (decidir/casarse)

15. Mientras nosotros _____ en tren, mi hermana _____

    por la ventana al desierto que _____ no tener límites, y yo

    _____ *Cien años de soledad*. (viajar/mirar/parecer/leer)

16. Recientemente, una persona me _____ que mi amigo

    _____ _____ una orca cuando él

    _____ por Puget Sound en su yate hace unos días.

    (informar/ver/navegar)

17. Juanito, ¿qué te _____ la maestra ayer que _____
    para tu proyecto final? (sugerir/hacer)

18. Ya que los soldados no _____ si _____ a vivir

    o morir, _____ muchos delitos. (saber/ir/cometer)

19. En esos días, ella _____ con salir con Juan, a pesar de que ella

    _____ que Juan _____ casado.

    (soñar/saber/estar)

20. Yo _____ la billetera en la mochila, porque no

    _____ que nadie la _____ fácilmente y me

    la _____. (poner/querer/ver/robar)

21. La mamá de Cristina siempre le _____ que _____
    con muchachos con malas intenciones. (prohibir/salir)

22. Ellos _____ deprimidos aun antes de que sus amigos les

    _____ lo que _____ _____

    la noche anterior. (sentirse/revelar/ocurrir)

23. Ellos me _____ que _____ la tienda

    temprano, pero después de la hora en que el tráfico de las hora pico

    normalmente _____. (sugerir/abrir/disminuir)

24. Al salir el sol esta mañana, _____ el gallo, lo cual nos

    _____. (cantar/despertar)

25. Oye, muchachos, ¿no _____ a María en la reunión, cuando Uds.

    _____ de vacaciones la semana pasada? (conocer/regresar)

26. Mientras nosotros _____ de San Francisco a Seattle en tren, y

_____ a las cartas, el conductor nos _____

que _____ una demora de treinta minutos en la próxima

estación para reabastecer el vagón de cocina. (viajar/jugar/informar/haber)

27. El fin de semana pasado, cuando mi hija _____ su gato al

veterinario para que lo _____, él le _____ que

no _____ nada grave. (llevar/examinar/decir/tener)

28. Yo _____ a invitarla a salir conmigo pero si ella

_____ a acompañarme, _____ que buscar a

otra muchacha para ir al baile. (ir/negarse/tener)

29. Alfredo y yo acabamos de hablar con mi esposa y le _____

_____ que él y yo _____ a trabajar todo el

sábado que viene para sacar la mala hierba del jardín. (prometer/ir)

30. Aunque las atletas de nuestra universidad _____ de lleno para

ganar este fin de semana, las chicas del otro equipo _____

mejor entrenadas y por eso temo que nosotros _____ a perder

esta vez. (meterse/estar/ir)

31. Las chicas _____ escuchar música latina porque

_____ más bailable. (preferir/ser)

32. ¿_____ tú que _____ obvio anoche que Juan

_____ celos de Enrique? (creer/ser/sentir)

33. Mi padre dice que _____ a la reunión esta noche, pero que si él

no _____ ir por alguna razón, _____ que tú

_____ por él. (asistir/poder/querer/ir)

34. Dijiste que ellos _____ el pastel, si tú _____ la
ensalada. (hacer/preparar)

35. Este fin de semana, los Caballeros Aztecas _____ explorar el

    valle, a menos que _____ demasiado frío. (pensar/hacer)

36. Creo que ayer, cuando _____ a la conferencia, los delegados ya

    _____ _____ todo lo que _____

    para tomar su decisión. (venir/oír/necesitar)

37. Dudo que cuando los delegados _____ a la conferencia ayer, ya

    _____ _____ todo lo que _____

    para tomar su decisión. (venir/oír/necesitar)

38. Tú y yo _____ a María cuando ella _____ la
    chaqueta para dar un paseo por el parque ayer. (ver/ponerse)

39. Cuando tú y mi hermana _____ para ir al almacén esta mañana,

    _____ _____ las tarjetas de crédito.

    (salir/olvidar)

40. Después de que _____ de llover, yo _____ a
    jugar al béisbol por un par de horas. (dejar/ir)

41. Tomás dijo que no lo _____ hasta que él lo _____
    con sus propios ojos. (creer/ver)

42. Una vez que Tomás lo _____ con sus propios ojos, lo

    _____. (ver/creer)

43. Hace poco, los tres arquitectos _____ que _____
    un museo cerca de los edificios gubernamentales. (proponer/construirse)

44. Anoche, los marineros _____ que _____

    _____ un velero misterioso que _____

    hacia el norte a toda vela. (decir/observar/navegar)

45. Esta mañana, cuando Uds. _____ que alguien _____

    _____ la ventana de la tienda, también _____

    evidencia de otro crimen. (ver/romper/descubrir)

46. Cuando Juan y Teresa _____ a las once anoche, los dos

    _____ en seguida. (acostarse/dormirse)

47. Esa noche, cuando yo _____, un anciano _____

    la puerta y _____ las luces de la gran biblioteca secreta. (llegar/

    abrir/encender)

48. Cuando nosotros _____ la película mañana, espero que

    nosotros _____ algo que antes no _____.

    (ver/aprender/saber)

49. Ahora que _____ _____ la lección, tú

    _____ que no _____ fácil, pero es cierto que

    la _____ mejor mañana. (leer/ver/ser/entender)

50. Ellos se conocieron y, aunque realmente no lo _____,

    _____ irresistiblemente. (querer/enamorarse)

Answer key

Keep in mind when checking your work in the translation exercises that as long as your solutions mean the same thing as the sentences given in the key, you are doing fine. It is inevitable that translations may vary, since meaning is more important than the exact words. When any doubt remains, focus on your rendition of the verbs.

1 The imperfect: Description and background

1·1
1. i
2. n
3. p
4. l
5. k
6. i
7. j
8. p
9. j
10. o
11. h
12. k
13. n
14. g
15. h
16. f
17. e
18. d
19. c
20. b
21. e
22. a

23. c

24. b

25. c

1·2

1. cantaba

2. comíamos

3. dormía, leía *Note that the subjects of the two verbs are different but that the first- and third-person singular endings are identical in form in the imperfect.*

4. trabajaba

5. era

6. estudiaba

7. escribía

8. visitaba

9. iban

10. observaban

11. sentía

12. podía, agradaba *Here,* **él** *is the subject of* **poder;** **la idea** *is the subject of* **agradar.**

13. conocía, salía *Here,* **yo** *is the subject of both verbs.*

14. veía

15. sabías

16. abría, esperaba *In this case, both subjects are third-person singular, but they represent different people.*

17. oías, mirabas *In this sentence, the subject of both verbs is* **tú.**

18. había

19. pensaba

20. quería

1·3

1. The children did not want to go home because they were having a lot of fun playing football (soccer).

2. The horses were galloping (galloped) over the pampas for several hours in search of water. *In English, the use of the single verb "galloped" is still understood as an ongoing action, but if one were translating in the other direction, this aspect would have to be reflected by using the imperfect, not the preterite. This observation applies to the other optional answers indicated in the key to this exercise.*

3. How did you feel (How were you feeling) when your daughter was going to get married?

4. While I was writing (wrote) these exercises, I was listening to Latin music.

5. I used to (would) surf for six hours every afternoon when I lived in Hawaii.

6. In order to become an expert pianist, she used to (would) practice every day.

7. My wife used to prepare (prepared, kept on preparing) many traditional dishes while we worked (were working) in the yard.

8. The work was very hard and we would drink a lot of water all day.

9. Although they used to catch him every time he crossed the border, he would return with the same determination.

10. Sometimes, that boy would beat me when we played chess./That boy sometimes beat me at the chess matches we used to play.

11. That couple used to dance all night, but now they are an old couple in love.

12. Little by little, we moved along, penetrating deeper into an unknown region of the Amazon jungle.

13. The moon was rising over an aquatic horizon to my right while I, at 21° N., contemplated the Big Dipper.

14. When I was a little boy, I had the bad habit of putting too much salt on my food.

15. In the Stone Age, there were no cars or airplanes.

1·4   1. Mientras viajaban por el desierto, veían los muchos tipos de cactus.

2. Eran alrededor de las dos de la mañana y leían. *Time of day is always expressed by the use of* **ser** *in the imperfect.*

3. ¿Comías solamente legumbres cuando vivías en la India?

4. Sus amigos creían que ella podía bailar bien.

5. Íbamos al cine casi todas las noches cuando vivíamos allí.

6. Mientras volábamos, ninguna de las asistentes de vuelo podía descansar.

7. Él preparaba la cena y ella mezclaba la ensalada.

8. Siempre cuando ellos venían a nuestra casa, jugábamos a los naipes hasta la medianoche.

9. Antes no había crimen en esta ciudad.

10. Cuando ellos tenían catorce o quince años, dormían en la playa.

11. A lo lejos, yo podía oír el tren que iba para Chicago.

12. Él leía pero ellos escribían.

13. Él era famoso. *Grammatically, it would make no difference if one used the preterite here (i.e.,* **Él fue famoso.**)*; aside from the fact that this is an exercise in the imperfect, however, it is worth observing that the imperfect invites elaboration while the preterite closes the subject.*

14. Había cinco personas en el restaurante anoche a las once.

15. ¿Querían ellos acompañarte?

2 The preterite: Narration, or what happened?

2·1

1. v
2. u
3. u
4. s
5. u
6. t
7. p
8. q
9. r
10. m
11. l
12. n
13. o
14. k
15. i
16. h
17. l
18. j
19. e
20. g
21. f
22. d
23. b
24. a
25. c

2·2

1. dijiste
2. conocí
3. tuvo
4. supo *Remember that* **saber** *in the preterite means* to find out something, *because the preterite refers to a specific action at a given time in the past.*
5. pagué
6. leyó

7. quiso *Remember that* **querer** *in the preterite means* to try *or, if negative, to* refuse, *because the preterite refers to a specific action at a given time in the past.*

8. diste

9. comimos

10. viste

11. pudo *Remember that* **poder** *in the preterite means* to succeed *or, if negative, to* fail to do something, *because the preterite refers to a specific action at a given time in the past.*

12. fue

13. comencé

14. tradujeron

15. pudo

16. trajimos

17. cantó

18. pusiste

19. quiso, quiso

20. fuiste

21. estuvieron

22. vino

23. busqué

24. vivieron

25. hablaron

2·3

1. The milk spoiled after so many days in the refrigerator.

2. The troops surrendered their weapons after losing the battle.

3. The tropical fish died from copper poisoning in the tank.

4. I refused to study chemistry in school.

5. His (*or* Her) parents insisted on going to see the Christmas play with the neighbors.

6. You accompanied her back to her house, didn't you?

7. The mother defended her son.

8. They ordered cake from the waiter.

9. My friends decided to open a bank account in Switzerland.

10. You looked for the dog for how many hours last night?

11. A lightning bolt struck it, which caused a fire that consumed the entire building.

12. He fell asleep in class.

13. To whom did you give the earrings, Maria or Christina?

14. They put him in jail for embezzlement.

15. I started to sing and my friends covered their ears.

16. We had an exam in geometry class this morning.

17. The little girl fell from the swing just a minute ago.

18. I met my wife in 1990.

19. They drove to San Diego, taking six-hour shifts for three days straight.

20. Who brought me this hat?

2·4
1. Fuimos a Vegas el mes pasado.

2. Ella y Teresa tradujeron este artículo.

3. Supe que ella es honesta cuando me dijo la verdad sobre su hermano.

4. ¿Quisiste abrir la puerta?

5. Él y yo regresamos (*or* volvimos) a casa muy tarde anoche.

6. Yo los busqué por una hora.

7. Ella no pudo arrancar el carro.

8. ¿Fueron tú y Juan a la cafetería esta mañana? *Or* **Fuisteis**, *in Spain, if using the familiar plural.*

9. Ella conoció a su esposo actual el pasado diciembre en la fiesta de Juanita.

10. Ellos rompieron la ventana.

11. La mesera nos sirvió la sangría y las tapas.

12. No pudimos encontrar (*or* hallar) la maleta.

13. Le pagué al taxista y subí (*or* fui) a mi cuarto de hotel.

14. Ellos trataron de (*or* quisieron) encontrarnos.

15. Empezó a llover tan pronto como empezó (*or* comenzó) el partido.

16. Ella y yo lo conocimos en el partido de fútbol.

17. No quisimos comprar el carro.

18. Ellos intentaron (*or* quisieron) escalar la montaña.

19. Él vio la película tres veces.

20. Ellos subieron las gradas de la catedral.

3 The imperfect and the preterite together: Narrating and describing in the past

3·1
1. llovía **Mientras** *always requires the imperfect since it means "while" or "meanwhile."*

2. corrió *At the time this sentence is spoken, the five-mile run is over and the speaker is not elaborating about anything that happened during the run.*

3. escribía *The speaker's and Juan's actions are being reported as actions that were going on at the same time.*

4. hiciste *The question refers to what someone did at a specific moment, after another action ended in the past.*

5. esperaba *Her waiting is going on at the same time as everyone else's doubt.*

6. supiste *There is only one first time for everything, hence the preterite of* **saber** *must be used when referring to* coming to know *something in the past.*

7. fue *The preterite of* **ser** *is used because the matter is being brought to a conclusion, hence it is summarizing or ending the discusssion.*

8. pudo *The negative of* **poder** *in the preterite means* to fail, *or* not to succeed.

9. iba *Little Red Riding Hood was picking flowers while she was going through the woods.*

10. podía *The speaker's capacity to do something is a given, although he or she did not follow through with action; hence the use of the imperfect is descriptive, not narrative.*

11. estaba *Both action and circumstance are contemporaneous.*

12. habló *Since Fidel spoke for seven hours, there is a stated end to the speech, hence the preterite is required.*

13. fuimos *The action of going refers to a specific instance.*

14. decidió *A moment of decision in the past is expressed by the preterite.*

15. miraban *Like* **mientras**, **durante** *also always requires the imperfect when used in the past.*

16. vieron *The preterite is needed when reporting something that happened suddenly.*

17. dijo *The teacher said something at a specific moment about what the little boy did last week.*

18. eran *The imperfect is used because the speaker is describing past circumstances.*

19. quiso *The preterite of* **querer** *shows an attempt to do something at a specific time in the past.*

20. puso *Mary put the book down at a specific moment. The action is over and done.*

21. prohibían *The use of* **siempre** *referring to the past always requires the imperfect.*

22. me sentía *The reporting of feelings, moods, or attitudes in the past is generally descriptive. When the preterite is used with such verbs, it shows a change.*

23. abrió *The action of opening is reported as finished.*

24. despertamos/despertó *The subjects' waking up, or being woken up, is reported as over, not as a process.*

25. conociste *One can only meet someone for the first time once, hence the preterite of* **conocer** *is used.*

3·2
1. leía, mirabas *Contemporaneous past actions.*

2. examinó, concluyó *Sequential, completed past actions.*

3. invité, quiso *Sequential, completed past actions.*

4. trabajó, descansó *Sequential, completed past actions.*

5. intentaron, lograron *Sequential, completed past actions.*

6. cantaban, bailaban *Contemporaneous past actions.*

7. Fue (*or* Era), estaba *The use of the preterite denotes an impression that was made at the moment while the imperfect denotes that the impression was ongoing.*

8. querían, pudieron *The verb* **querer** *is used to express a mental state in the past, but* **poder** *is used in the preterite showing that the desire was thwarted.*

9. hacía, preparabas *Contemporaneous past actions.*

10. quiso, pudo *Sequential, completed past actions: an attempt was made but failed.*

11. escuchaba, apuntaba *Contemporaneous past actions.*

12. compraban, llevaban *Habitual past actions.*

13. viste, corrías *Running is the circumstance in which the person saw Mary.*

14. iba, veía *Contemporaneous past actions: the speaker's sister was going to school and it was foggy, so the park could not be seen.*

15. llovió, jugó *Sequential, completed past actions.*

16. creía, vio *Thomas's disbelief was a mental state until something happened: he saw with his own eyes.*

17. caminaban, recogían *Contemporaneous past actions.*

18. construyeron, vendieron *Sequential, completed past actions.*

19. deseaba, podía *Contemporaneous past actions, both showing circumstances, one mental (the young woman's desire to go to the party), one external (her parents' stating that she was unable to go).*

20. navegó, llegó *Sequential past actions.*

21. me desperté, me levanté *Sequential past actions.*

22. abrió, encendió *Sequential past actions.*

23. leímos, supimos *Sequential past actions.*

24. cerraste, apagaste *Sequential past actions.*

25. Subió, empezó *Sequential past actions.*

26. vio, se enamoró *Sequential past actions.*

3·3

1. The workers opened the bridge as soon as the boat arrived.

2. My friends were eating pizza but I preferred to study.

3. His girlfriend decided to break up with him because she did not like his cigarettes.

4. While we were going to the bank, we found out on the radio that someone was holding it up.

5. The football (soccer) fans tried to enter the stadium, but the guards did not let them pass.

6. Couldn't you finish the homework? What is wrong? It's just that you refused to study, isn't it?

7. Several weeks went by and she finally answered him with a long letter, explaining to him that she did not want to marry him, but rather someone else.

8. While the children were playing in the yard, their mother went up to the bedroom to try to sleep, but she couldn't.

9. The firemen arrived at the fire and quickly put it out.

10. While we were flying from Madrid to New York, we watched a movie.

11. The children got dressed, went out to play, and only came back when the sun was going down.

12. It was a fantastic day: it was neither hot nor cold, it wasn't cloudy, and I didn't have anything to do.

13. When John was eight years old, his family moved from Mexico City to San Antonio.

14. The roads were closed for several days, and when they opened them, no one could drive on them because of the fallen trees.

15. At the moment her parents entered, her boyfriend jumped out the window and ran off.

16. Every thunderclap made the windows rattle; the cold could be felt entering from under the doors when, suddenly, the door seemed to open of its own accord and a dark figure entered.

17. It was four o'clock when we left work, but we couldn't get home until nine because of the traffic.

18. The submarine dove until it was 2,000 feet below sea level, then remained still for several hours.

19. The politicians went on speaking for hours and, as always, no one believed them.

20. At the party last night, the girls started dancing but the guys kept on eating.

21. How old were you when your parents gave you permission to go to the movies alone?

22. The dog was sleeping when the cat ate up all his food.

23. When I woke up, breakfast was already ready.

24. We could smell the coffee when we entered the restaurant.

25. When my father arrived, it was eight o'clock in the evening.

26. There were a lot of people who wanted to attend the concert but many could not go because there were not enough seats.

3·4   1. ¿Dónde estaban tus amigos cuando regresaste a casa anoche?

2. El chofer dormía cuando perdió control del auto.

3. ¿Qué hora era cuando viniste a mi casa?

4. ¿Iba ella a la fiesta cuando empezó a llover?

5. Terminaste la novela después de que yo llegué.

6. Los niños no sabían vestirse.

7. ¿Qué hiciste el fin de semana pasado?

8. Cuando ella supo lo que pasaba en la escuela, llamó a sus amigos.

9. ¿Quisiste conocerlo cuando vino a visitarnos?

10. Nevaba la semana pasada pero no hacía mucho frío.

11. Ellos (*or* Ellas) aprendieron a leer cuando tenían siete años.

12. Ella tenía veintisiete años cuando nos conocimos.

13. Ella se puso el abrigo y salió de la casa, aunque llovía.

14. Él quiso vender la casa, pero no pudo.

15. No quise dejar a mi perro solo cuando me fui de vacaciones el mes pasado.

16. Ella me conoció en la universidad el año pasado.

17. Ellos (*or* Ellas) siempre iban de compras juntos (*or* juntas), pero nunca compraban nada.

18. Yo quería ver la película, pero no pude ir.

19. Ella quiso asistir a clase pero no pudo ir.

20. Ellos (*or* Ellas) querían ir al zoológico, pero tuvieron que quedarse en casa.

21. Mi familia iba a la playa los fines de semana.

22. Cuando él supo que ella había salido con su mejor amigo, no quiso creerlo.

23. Ellos (*or* Ellas) miraban la tele cuando se apagaron las luces.

24. Él y yo cocinábamos mucho.

25. Teresa y Marta querían llamarme, pero su teléfono no funcionaba.

26. La madre de mi amigo hablaba por teléfono cuando yo quise llamarlo.

3·5   **A.**

1. pensaban (*or* creían)

2. había

3. sabía

4. descubrió

5. creía (*or* pensaba)

6. murió

7. encontró (*or* descubrió)

8. era

9. murió

10. aprendieron

11. Fue

B.

1. volvían

2. gustaba

3. hacía

4. querían
5. sabían
6. iban
7. llegaron
8. jugaban
9. vieron
10. había
11. supieron
12. podía
13. estaba
14. oyeron
15. querían
16. preferían (*or* prefirieron)
17. Eran
18. llegaron

4   The present perfect: What have you done for me lately?

4·1
1. V
2. PA
3. TP
4. A
5. A
6. V
7. V
8. V
9. PA
10. TP
11. V
12. TP
13. TP
14. V
15. A
16. V
17. PA
18. V

19. TP
20. PA

4·2
1. ha escrito
2. he visto
3. han corrido
4. ha sido
5. he hecho
6. se han muerto
7. han ido
8. has comido
9. ha dado
10. me he puesto
11. hemos abierto
12. os habéis acostado
13. me he acostado
14. has dicho
15. se ha dedicado
16. ha roto
17. he vuelto
18. has creído
19. han resuelto
20. hemos imprimido

4·3
1. Our plow has broken.
2. She has not told her boyfriend the truth.
3. Having seen the spectacle, they left the tent.
4. Due to the storm, a huge tree has fallen in the park.
5. She has married John.
6. The children are tired because they have played all afternoon.
7. So, I have not seen a marvel because I have never gone to Seville.
8. There have been so many people who have been imprisoned recently that there is a new prison built in another nearby town.
9. Has your friend done the homework?
10. We have the house open from four in the afternoon until six, during the summer.

11. I have put a new flamenco CD in the CD player so I can listen to it.
12. They say that the problem has been solved, but that the broken machine is still at the construction site.
13. The concert has begun.
14. Pandora has opened the box.
15. That neighbor couple that used to fight so much has broken up.
16. Have you ever seen such affrontery?
17. We have heard a lot about that politician and he does not impress us.
18. The boxer has fallen for the third time.
19. I don't know what you have done, but it has caused a lot of problems.
20. Maria has fallen madly in love with him.

4·4
1. He visto el partido en la tele hoy.
2. Sus jefes le han dado un aumento de sueldo.
3. Ellos siempre han vivido en esta ciudad.
4. Has hecho todo el trabajo.
5. He puesto los papeles en la mesa.
6. Mi madre ha preparado una cena fantástica.
7. ¿Adónde ha ido mi perro?
8. El periódico ha sido impreso.
9. Hemos escrito una carta a nuestros/los abuelos.
10. Los niños se han puesto los zapatos, ¡por fin!
11. Ella se ha roto la pierna. No debe esquiar.
12. Él ha competido con su hermano desde que estaban en la secundaria.
13. Ella se ha vestido para ir al baile.
14. Ellos han imprimido el periódico.
15. Las modelos se han maquillado y están listas para exhibir los nuevos estilos.
16. El carro se ha chocado con el árbol.
17. Su abuelo se ha muerto.
18. Su relación se ha acabado.
19. Ella ha perdido las llaves.
20. Susana ha dicho una mentira.

4·5
1. La maestra nos ha traído el pastel. La maestra nos lo ha traído.
2. El gato se ha comido el pájaro. El gato se lo ha comido.

3. Les hemos escrito las cartas a nuestros clientes. Se las hemos escrito.

4. Los gerentes le han dado un ascenso y un aumento de sueldo. Los gerentes se los han dado.

5. El taxista me ha llevado a mi hotel favorito.

6. Las secretarias/Los secretarios han puesto los documentos en el archivo. Las secretarias/Los secretarios los han puesto en el archivo.

7. He escuchado la canción. La he escuchado.

8. El juez se ha muerto.

9. Le has dicho la verdad a ella. Se la has dicho.

10. Hemos sabido lo que ella le ha hecho a él.

11. ¿Han leído Uds. las noticias? ¿Las han leído?

12. Ellos han tratado de comprar las acciones. Ellos las han tratado de comprar./Ellos han tratado de comprarlas.

13. ¿Qué les has dicho?

14. Ella ha roto el juguete. Ella lo ha roto.

15. ¿Han arreglado la computadora? ¿La han arreglado?

16. He vuelto/regresado a la ciudad.

17. Mis amigos me han enviado/mandado un regalo. Mis amigos me lo han enviado/mandado.

18. Ellos se han ido a pescar.

19. Susana y Juan han roto relaciones. Susana y Juan las han roto.

20. La he visto en la tienda de comestibles.

5   The pluperfect: What happened before something else

5·1
1. j
2. c
3. h
4. m
5. i
6. g
7. d
8. f
9. k
10. n
11. o
12. k
13. a

14. e

15. l

5·2 1. había dicho

2. había visto

3. había dado

4. se habían mudado

5. habían querido

6. me había puesto

7. se había ido

8. habían mirado

9. había enviado

10. se habían roto

11. había escrito

12. había absuelto

13. habían pagado

14. habían leído

15. había vendido

16. habían venido

17. habíamos hecho

18. había comido

19. se había caído

20. habían examinado

5·3 1. When the monkey arrived at the foot of the tree, the tiger had already arrived.

2. The astronauts discovered that someone had arrived on the planet before them!

3. He hurried to get to the hospital on time, but his wife had already given birth when he arrived.

4. The captain of the expedition had died before arriving at the river's source.

5. When the first humans appeared in Africa, the dinosaurs had already disappeared.

6. When they found out what was happening with the economy, it was late; they had put their funds in fixed bonds that they were not going to be able to sell for five years.

7. Cervantes had died when his novel *Persiles* was published in 1616.

8. I went to the shop at eight, but the owners had not opened it.

9. Columbus cannot be considered the discoverer of the New World since, when he arrived, it had been millennia since the Amerindians had discovered it.

10. We had solved the problem with the car when the mechanic came.

11. According to some doctors, when someone says that an old man fell and broke his hip, it's because his hip had broken already, causing him to fall.

12. When Thomas sent the letter, his girlfriend had already gone on vacation.

13. The parents told their children that the gifts were from the Three Kings, but they had already seen them under the bed.

14. We wanted to know if the cake for the party had been made yet.

15. Someone had burglarized the house because we saw that the window had been broken from outside and the front door had been opened from within, which is how the burgler got out, no doubt.

16. When the professor mentioned the idea to me, I realized that I had never thought of it.

17. His wife wanted to speak to him for a while more, but he had fallen asleep.

18. Several people arrived at the inn but the kitchen had closed.

19. The children wanted to swim but the sun had set already.

20. When I finished this exercise, it was three in the morning and I had not gone to sleep.

5·4

1. La cena ya estaba lista pero los niños no se habían lavado las manos.

2. Escalamos la montaña para ver la salida del sol, pero ya había salido.

3. Habían nacido los gatitos antes de la fiesta del sábado.

4. Él había decidido informarle a ella antes del martes sobre el viaje.

5. Cuando ella lo llamó, él ya había invitado a su hermana al baile.

6. Ellos volvieron a casa a las nueve, pero la película ya había terminado.

7. Él quería sorprenderla pero ella ya había visto la sortija.

8. Los niños habían abierto la ventana antes de la tormenta.

9. Ella no le había dicho nada sobre su otro novio cuando él los vio en el restaurante.

10. Cuando colgamos el teléfono, yo todavía no había encontrado el artículo.

11. El tren llegaba y todavía no habían abierto la estación.

12. Él no se había muerto cuando terminó la guerra.

13. Cuando sus abuelos vinieron a los EE.UU., él no había nacido todavía.

14. Mi amigo se había mudado antes de recibir la carta.

15. El artículo había sido escrito antes del domingo pasado.

16. Ella se había puesto el abrigo cuando se dio cuenta de que no hacía frío.

17. Mi amigo y yo no habíamos visto el mar hasta que teníamos diez años.

18. Él no había oído hablar de ese conjunto musical hasta que vio un artículo sobre ellos en una revista.

19. Cuando él volvió de la guerra, supo que su novia se había casado.

20. ¿Habías leído los informes antes de reunirse el comité?

6 The conditional: What would be and the future of the past

6·1
1. j
2. m
3. s
4. a
5. l
6. p
7. c
8. o
9. n
10. t
11. f
12. r
13. i
14. h
15. g
16. k
17. b
18. q
19. e
20. d

6·2
1. sabría
2. asistirías
3. creería
4. traería
5. gustaría
6. encontraríamos
7. podrían

8. trabajaríamos

9. tendrían

10. habría *When used to express* there is, are, were, *etc., the verb* **haber** *is always singular.*

11. diría

12. pondría

13. venderían

14. saldría

15. harías

16. Serían

17. iríamos

18. llegarían

19. daría

20. querría

6·3

1. The children would set the table if their mother asked them to.

2. If it weren't for your parents, you wouldn't be here.

3. The professor told her she would learn a lot in his class.

4. If you wanted, you could go with me to the movies, to see that actor you say I look like!

5. That guy told me that he would come look for me around six, but he has not come.

6. Where could my mother have been when her cousin called her?

7. What would my wife say to me if I called her "my heaven"?

8. Maria must have been writing poetry last night because she is in love with him.

9. I would dance more if my knee didn't hurt.

10. If all mothers-in-law died, husbands would be worth more.

11. We would like to teach a class together if we could find an interesting subject.

12. She told her little boy that she would give him a bath soon.

13. Would you be interested in traveling to Paris if the airline gave you a free ticket?

14. I promised my students that I would play more music in class.

15. If I played Cuban music, would the students dance?

16. Could you help me pick the songs for class?

17. Students ought to attend class every day.

6·4

1. Ella iría a la fiesta si tuviera tiempo.

2. Ellos dijeron que traerían la comida.

3. Él me dijo que ella encontraría el número de teléfono del gerente.

4. Ellos estarían en la librería cuando llamé.

5. ¿Qué me diría si pudiera verme ahora?

6. ¿Cómo dirías "It's a beautiful day" en español?

7. Si Juan fuera más alto, le pediríamos que jugara en nuestro equipo.

8. Cuando su novio regresó a casa, ella estaría estudiando.

9. Él estaría contento cuando la vio anoche.

10. ¿Qué harías si ganaras la lotería?

11. Mi amigo dijo que leería más si tuviera tiempo.

12. Si no fuera por la diferencia de edad, su situación sería diferente.

13. Yo estaría cocinando cuando me llamaste.

14. Aun si el precio de las casas subiera mucho, no vendería la mía.

15. El carro iría demasiado rápido.

16. Si tuviera un caballo, lo llamaría Sirocco.

17. El médico me dijo que no me operaría la rodilla.

18. Los niños jugarían cuando empezó a llover. (*or* estarían jugando)

19. Si yo fuera francés, pensaría de manera diferente sobre la vida.

20. Yo comería más pescado si no costara tanto.

7 The conditional perfect: What would have been

7·1
1. o
2. k
3. t
4. i
5. j
6. a
7. q
8. b
9. r
10. s
11. c
12. d
13. e
14. m
15. g
16. p

17. l

18. h

19. n

20. f

7·2   1. habría sabido

2. habrías asistido

3. habría creído

4. traería

5. gustaría

6. habríamos encontrado

7. podrían

8. habríamos trabajado

9. habrían tenido

10. habrían abandonado

11. habría dicho

12. habría puesto

13. habrían vendido

14. habría salido

15. habrías hecho

16. Habría sido

17. habríamos ido

18. habrían llegado

19. habría dado

20. habría querido

7·3   1. The children would have set the table if their mother had asked them to.

2. If it had not been for your parents, you would not have been born, of course.

3. The professor told her that she would have learned a lot in his class if she had dedicated herself to her studies.

4. If you had wanted, you would have been able to go with me to the movies that night, to see the actor you say I look like!

5. That young man confessed to me that he would have come for me around six, but that he couldn't because his car broke down.

6. We were wondering where my mother could have been when she finally came home.

7. What would my wife have said to me if I had called her "my heaven" when she was angry?

8. Maria would probably have written poetry that summer because she was in love with him.

9. I would have danced more if my knee had not hurt so much.

10. If mothers-in-law had all died, husbands would have been worth more.

11. We would have liked to teach a class together that year if we had been able to find an interesting subject.

12. She told her little boy that she would have bathed him but there was not enough hot water.

13. Would you have been interested in traveling to Paris last fall if the airline had given you a free ticket?

14. I assured the students that I would have played more music in class if it hadn't been for the class across the hall.

15. If I had played Cuban music, would the students have danced?

16. Would you have been able to help me select the songs for class if we had been able to play them?

17. The students would have attended class every day if it had not been for the many distractions of the city.

7·4

1. Ella habría ido a la fiesta si hubiera tenido tiempo.

2. Ellos dijeron que habrían traído (*or* llevado) la comida, pero que no tenían suficiente dinero.

3. Él nos dijo que ella habría encontrado el número de teléfono del gerente si no hubiera perdido su bolsa.

4. Ellos habrían estado en la librería, porque cuando les llamé, mencionaron que habían encontrado una novela interesante.

5. ¿Qué habría dicho ella si hubiera podido verme entonces?

6. ¿Cómo habrías dicho "It's a beautiful day" en español?

7. Si Juan hubiera sido más alto, le habríamos pedido que jugara en nuestro equipo.

8. Ella habría estado estudiando cuando regresó a casa su novio, porque sus libros estaban en la mesa.

9. Él la habría estado esperando toda la noche.

10. ¿Qué habrías hecho si hubieras ganado la lotería?

11. Mi amigo dijo que habría leído más si hubiera tenido tiempo cuando era niño.

12. Si no hubiera sido por la diferencia de edad, su situación habría sido diferente.

13. Cuando tú lo llamaste, él estaría cocinando porque hablaba mucho de la cena.

14. Aun si el precio de las casas hubiera subido mucho, no habría vendido la mía.

15. El carro habría estado yendo demasiado rápido.

16. Si hubiera tenido un caballo, lo habría llamado Sirroco.

17. El médico me dijo que no me habría operado la rodilla si no me hubiera dolido tanto.

18. Los niños habrían estado jugando toda la mañana cuando empezó a llover.

19. Si yo hubiera sido francés, habría pensado de manera diferente sobre la vida.

20. Yo habría comido más pescado si hubiera sabido que era tan sano.

8 The sequence of tenses: Observations on the indicative and the subjunctive

8·1

1. podían, tenían *Contemporaneous past actions: the dogs were in a condition of being unable to concentrate because they were hungry.*

2. esperaban, fueran *The past time frame is stated at the end of the sentence: yesterday. The main clause is a verb of wishing, introducing a subordinated clause in which, therefore, the verb must be in the imperfect subjunctive.*

3. dijo, viera *The time frame is set by the verb **era** in the subordinated clause, thus revealing that the main verb had to be in the preterite (not the imperfect indicative, because the verb **decir** is used to refer to one moment of speaking in the past). The last verb, in the imperfect subjunctive, is in the clause subordinated to the second subordinated clause **era importante que**. In other words, the first clause is not the one that causes the subjunctive to be necessary in the third clause, since the first clause employs the verb **decir** in its primary meaning of saying, not telling.*

4. dije, era, leyera *This sentence is a parallel of the previous one in terms of the types of clauses and their relationships to one another.*

5. Quieres, paguen *Contemporaneous present actions as defined by the word **ahora**.*

6. estudia, pueda *There is a reference to a future time, thus the present indicative is used in the main, or independent, clause and the present subjunctive is used in the subordinated clause.*

7. mencionó, habían publicado, dudé, hubieran traducido *The time frame is established by the temporal adverb **ayer**. The publication of the book is prior to that moment of speaking, hence the pluperfect indicative is used to report it. The speaker reports his or her response with the preterite, since the doubt came to mind when John mentioned it. The pluperfect subjunctive must be used in the subordinated clause introduced by the verb of doubt in the past because the speaker is doubtful that the book had been published prior to 2000.*

8. Es, has escrito *This is a straightforward declaration of what the speaker perceives, all indicative. The present perfect is used to show the action of writing as having commenced in 2006 and continued up to the moment of speaking.*

9. quiere, diga *Since no time frame is provided, the key has used the present tense only, indicative and subjunctive respectively. If the speaker were referring to the past, the verbs would be **quería**, **dijera**.*

10. pidió, cantáramos *The phrase **el fin de semana pasado** sets the action in the past. The subjunctive is used because the subordinated clause is introduced by a verb of requesting in the main clause.*

11. creo, es, trabajes *Since there is no indication of a past time, the present tense is used in the key. However, if the speaker were referring to the past, the verbs would have been **creía** (or **creí**), **era**, **trabajaras**. In this latter case, the choice of imperfect or preterite for the first verb depends*

only on whether the belief was an attitude the speaker held or an impression made at some moment in the past. The second verb would be in the imperfect indicative because of the expression of emotion, in the past.

12. gustaba, hubiéramos renunciado *The time frame is the past. The verb* **gustar** *is in the imperfect because it refers not to an instant impression of disliking but to a situation. The phrase* **antes de la Navidad** *is what makes the pluperfect subjunctive necessary.*

8·2

1. a *The main verb is in the past and is a verb of wanting.*

2. d *The main verb is a verb in the past used to merely report a previous action, hence no subjunctive can be used and that previous action is expressed with the pluperfect indicative.*

3. a *The main clause is in the past and introduces a subordinated adjective clause describing a beach that was not yet known to the subjects, hence the imperfect subjunctive must be used.*

4. c *The recommendation has been made regarding the future, hence the present subjunctive is used.*

5. b *The main clause introduces a subordinated clause describing a nonexistent antecedent and is in the past, therefore the imperfect subjunctive must be used.*

6. c *The main verb is in the past and the adverbial clause* **antes de que** *always requires the subjunctive, hence the imperfect subjunctive in the subordinated clause.*

7. b *There is an element of anticipation established by the phrase* **iba a ir** *and since it is in the past, the imperfect subjunctive must be used in the clause it introduces.*

8. a *The time frame established by the main verb is the past. The conditional in the subordinated clause expresses the consequence of a hypothetical action, which must be expressed by the imperfect subjunctive.*

9. d *The time frame is the future and the adverbial expression* **a menos que** *always requires the subjunctive, hence the present subjunctive must be used.*

10. b *The conditional perfect expresses the consequence of a hypothetical past action, which must be expressed by the pluperfect subjunctive.*

8·3

1. nieva, voy *The present time frame is revealed by the use of* **ahora**, *so the only challenge in this sentence is that of subject and verb agreement. The subject of verbs expressing weather phenomena is an abstract third person, such as Mother Nature.*

2. nadar, decidieron *The only admissible form of a verb that immediately follows a preposition is the infinitive. Because of the verb* **decidir**, *the sentence makes more sense in the past, unless one thinks of this decision to run five miles as a habitual action in the present,* **deciden**; *in the past,* **decidían**).

3. escribe, mira *The use of* **generalmente**, *without any reference to past time, makes this sentence most likely a statement of a general truth, hence the present. If there were an explicit reference to a past time frame, the use of* **generalmente** *would require the use of the imperfect indicative (***escribía, miraba***).*

4. dijo, hicieras *The past time frame is revealed by* **quería**; **decir** *is used in the sense of to say, not to tell, so the need for the imperfect subjunctive of* **hacer** *depends on* **quería**.

5. pensaba, sabía, vería *The use of* **murió** *sets the sentence in the past. The phrase* **todas las noches** *makes the imperfect of* **pensar** *necessary and the conditional of* **ver** *is an example of this tense's use as the future of the past.*

6. estaban, supiste *The imperfect inquires about the circumstance in the past when a person first learned of an accident.*

7. es, fue *The use of* **ahora** *shows that we are talking about what is obvious now. Since John Lennon is dead, and this is a summarizing statement about him, the preterite of* **ser** *is used in the second clause.*

8. quisieran, pudieron *The time frame is revealed at the end of the sentence. The phrase* **por mucho que** *therefore requires the imperfect subjunctive, and the preterite of* **poder**, *in the negative, shows that the climbers failed to reached the mountain's summit.*

9. había dicho, hiciera, iba, recogía *The use of the pluperfect for the verb* **decir** *establishes the chronology of events in the past: first, her mother told her not to do something, which she then went along doing, going through the woods and picking flowers (two contemporaneous past actions).*

10. habría hecho, hubiera tenido *This is a past hypothesis or counterfactual statement, hence the correlative construction using the conditional perfect and the pluperfect subjunctive.*

11. buscábamos, estaría, encontramos, buscamos *The adverb* **ayer** *sets the action in the past and refers to a repeated action. The conditional is used to show probability in the past and the two preterites are used to report a completed action and its result.*

12. hablaba, daba *Since Castro no longer gives speeches, and the statement is descriptive, both verbs are in the imperfect.*

13. se ponía, nos dimos, teníamos, fuimos *The word* **mientras** *in the past (indicated by* **ese día**) *requires the imperfect. The preterite thus is the most logical choice for* **darse cuenta**. *The imperfect is used to show a condition and the preterite to show the action taken.*

14. decidió, se casaría *Amaranta finally made a decision, hence the preterite. The conditional is used in its function as the future of the past.*

15. viajábamos, miraba, parecía, leía *This sentence makes the most sense interpreted in the past, although there is no explicit reference to a past time. All the actions are contemporaneous, hence the imperfect indicative. If interpreted as a statement about the present:* **viajamos**, **mira**, **parece**, **leo**.

16. informó, había visto, navegaba *When the person informed the speaker, the friend had already seen the orca, hence the pluperfect indicative. The imperfect indicative is used to establish the past circumstances under which the whale sighting happened.*

17. sugirió, hicieras *The past-tense, indicative verb of recommending in the main clause requires the imperfect subjunctive to be used in the subordinated noun clause.*

18. sabían, iban, cometieron (or cometían) *The first imperfect verb describes the circumstance. The second is another way of showing the future of the past and the last verb, if in the preterite, summarizes the soldiers' actions, while if it is in the imperfect, would suggest that more information is about to be offered.*

19. soñaba, sabía, estaba *All the verbs refer to contemporaneous past actions.*

20. puse, quería, viera, robara *The preterite is used to report a simple past action, the imperfect to introduce the two things the subject did not want to happen. The last two verbs are in the imperfect subjunctive because they are both subordinated to* **quería**.

21. prohibía, saliera *The mother's prohibition was a continual one. The second verb is in the subordinated clause and hence must be in the imperfect subjunctive. If understood as a present situation:* **prohibe**, **salga**.

22. se sentían, revelaran, había ocurrido *The past time frame is established by the last phrase. The first verb is imperfect since it expresses a mental state in the past. The subjunctive is always used after* **antes de que**, *and in this case is in a past time frame, hence the imperfect subjunctive. The pluperfect indicative is necessary to clarify the chronology.*

23. sugirieron, abriera, disminuía *The verb of suggesting requires the use of the subjunctive in the subordinated clause. The adversative conjunction* **pero** *ends the influence of that verb and thus the last verb is in the imperfect indicative, stating a general truth about traffic congestion at some period in the past. If understood as a present situation:* **sugieren**, **abra**, **disminuye**.

24. cantó, despertó *The preterite is used to show a series of past actions.*

25. conocieron, regresaron *The preterite is used to show a series of past actions.*

26. viajábamos, jugábamos, informó, habría *The two verbs in the imperfect refer to two contemporaneous past actions. The preterite indicates an action that happened in that situation and the conditional is used in its function of showing the future in the past.*

27. llevó, examinara, dijo, tenía *The preterite refers to a one-time event in the past; the imperfect subjunctive is required because of the purpose clause* **para que**. *The second use of the preterite refers to another finished action and the imperfect refers to the cat's condition.*

28. iba, se negara, tendría *The imperfect of the formula* **ir** + **a** + *infinitive in the imperfect is used as another way of expressing the future when in the past. The imperfect subjunctive is required because it is used in the if-clause of a hypothetical statement, the consequence of which is expressed with the conditional. If understood as a present situation:* **voy**, **se niega**, **tendré**.

29. hemos prometido, vamos *The present perfect shows that the action of speaking began in the past and its effect (a promise) continues in force. The promised action is still in the future from the time frame of the sentence.*

30. se meten (*or* se metan), están, vayamos *After* **aunque**, *either the indicative or subjunctive can be used, indicating certainty or to suggest a degree of doubt. The second verb is in the present indicative because it is a simple assertion of fact. The last verb is in the present subjunctive because the subordinated noun clause in which it appears is introduced by a verb of emotion.*

31. prefieren, es *Both verbs are in the present indicative because they make simple assertions.*

32. Creías (*or* Crees), era (*or* fue), sentía *The past time frame is established by* **anoche**, *and* **ser** *could be either in the imperfect indicative, to express a general impression, or in the preterite, to show a change of impression. The last verb is in the imperfect indicative because it purports to describe an emotional state in the past.*

33. asistirá, puede, quiere, vayas *The meeting is future relative to the moment of speaking. The next two verbs are in the present indicative because they express current circumstances. The last verb is in the present subjunctive because it is introduced by a verb of wanting.*

34. harían, prepararas *The conditional is used both in its function as the future of the past and to show the consequence of the action in the if-clause, which is expressed by the imperfect subjunctive.*

35. piensan, haga *The subjunctive must be used after **a menos que** and the time frame is the present, hence the present subjunctive.*

36. vinieron, habían oído, necesitaban *Although the sentence begins with the present, the verb **creer** is used to indicate the speaker's current belief about past events. The delegates arrived and had already heard all that they needed. The last verb is in the imperfect indicative because it describes the mental readiness of the delegates.*

37. vinieron, hubieran oído, necesitaban *This sentence, a permutation of the previous one, introduces the situation with a verb of doubt instead of belief. The doubt is not about the arrival of the delegates, hence that verb is still in the preterite of the indicative. The doubt is cast on whether they had heard what they needed, hence the pluperfect subjunctive. Note that there is no doubt cast on whether the information that they needed exists, hence the last verb is still in the imperfect indicative.*

38. vimos, se ponía (*or* se puso) *The usage of the imperfect and the preterite is explained by the fact that Maria was in the act of putting on her coat when the subjects saw her.*

39. salieron, habían olvidado *The subjects left without the credit cards, therefore the forgetting happened prior to their departure, hence the pluperfect to express their omission.*

40. dejó, fui *The preterite is used to express two sequential actions in the past.*

41. creería, viera *The conditional is used both in its function as a future of the past and to express the consequence of a hypothetical action, although here that action is not stated in an if-clause but in an adverbial clause that either anticipates a future event (seeing with his own eyes), or admits it as possible.*

42. vio, creyó *The preterite is used to express two sequential actions in the past.*

43. propusieron, se construyera *The main verb is a verb of recommendation in the preterite, requiring that the imperfect subjunctive be used in the subordinated clause.*

44. dijeron, habían observado, navegaba *The preterite is used because the sailors' speaking is completed. The pluperfect indicates an occurrence prior to that moment of speaking and the imperfect shows the circumstance in which their observation took place.*

45. vieron, había roto, descubrieron *The preterite is used to show that the action of seeing is regarded as complete. Prior to the subjects' seeing, the damage had been done, hence the pluperfect. The last verb is in the preterite because it expresses a second sequential action in the past (following **vieron**). The subjects first saw the broken window, and then discovered evidence of an additional crime.*

46. se acostaron, se durmieron *The preterite is used to express two sequential past actions.*

47. llegué, abrió, encendió *The preterite is used to express three sequential past actions.*

48. veamos, aprendamos, sabíamos *The viewing of the movie is future relative to the present moment of speaking. Hence, the action expressed by the verb following **cuando** is anticipated and therefore the present subjunctive is needed. The second use of the present subjunctive, however, is due to its being introduced by a verb of wishing in the present indicative. The last verb is in the imperfect indicative because it follows the adverb **antes**.*

49. has leído, ves, era, entenderás *The temporal clues in the sentence make these the only reasonable forms. No subjunctives are necessary.*

50. quisieron, se enamoraron *The past time frame is established by* **conocieron**. *The preterite of* **querer** *is the most reasonable, since it is stated that the couple fell in love almost against their will. The preterite of* **enamorarse** *is used simply because the focus is on the past action, not the process of falling in love.*